The Complete Book of
BEDROOM
ELEGANCE

The Complete Book of
BEDROOM ELEGANCE

With over 30 projects for the bedroom of your dreams

Lady Caroline Wrey

THE OVERLOOK PRESS
WOODSTOCK • NEW YORK

Acknowledgements

I would like to thank George, my husband, for all his love, never-ending support and constant enthusiasm over the production of this second book. In addition, I would have found it extremely hard to write without the brilliant guidance and expertise of my editor, Margot Richardson. I am also deeply grateful for the unstinting support from Julian Shuckburgh and Mary Scott at Ebury Press. Equally, Pauline Graham's skills and knowledge have been wonderful. I also want to thank Mrs Martin Elwes for allowing us to use her master bedroom, and David Sassoon of Belville Sassoon, for lending the beautiful yellow suit – both for the back jacket photograph.

First published in 1994 by
The Overlook Press
Lewis Hollow Road
Woodstock, New York 12498

Library of Congress Cataloging-in-Publication Data

Wrey, Caroline, 1957-
    The complete book of bedroom elegance / Lady Caroline Wrey.
        p. cm.
    Includes bibliographical references and index.
    1. House furnishings. 2. Sewing. 3. Bedrooms. 4. Interior decoration. I. Title.
    TT387.W74   1994
    646.2'1-dc20

ISBN : 0-87951-509-0

                                                              92-23163
                                                                 CIP

Contents

INTRODUCTION

I have always been passionate about sewing, ever since I was quite young.

I believe I must have started at about the age of three, learning on lovely coloured sewing cards, using different coloured wools threaded through a huge tapestry needle (firmly knotted at its eye so it didn't come undone after every stitch).

Later, when I was about five years old, my mother taught me how to embroider dear little mats using 'Binca' rectangles or squares, and ordinary smocking skeins of every colour. Learning how to do basic embroidery stitches was very satisfying. My mother would then back the mat for me in a pretty gingham check (to cover up the untidy backs of the stitches) and it would make a perfect Christmas present for my grandmother or aunt.

I also clearly remember making a small needle book out of felt, green on the outside and cream inside, with yellow blanket-stitch edges and my mother's initials in chain stitch on the front. A perfect present, and treasured to this day, which is lovely.

As well, I made and embroidered a book-cover for my grandmother's diary. She has kept a diary every year since she was twelve – and she was born in 1895.

Later, I started dressmaking: a basic A-line skirt where every stitch had to be done by hand – even the side seams. (All that dreadful back stitching.) Then, at my boarding-school we had a brilliant sewing teacher and we were allowed to sew at weekends. We all took a great deal of pride in our work, and winning the sewing prizes was hugely satisfying. Leaving school, and being able to make my own clothes was a joy, since I was able to make all sorts of wonderful (and inexpensive) clothes for parties.

There are lots of other hobbies I adore – skiing, riding, tennis – but sewing gives me some of the greatest pleasure in life. It is hard to describe the depth of contentment when I finish a smocked dress for my daughter, Rachel, or a pair of tartan knickerbockers for one of my boys, Harry and Humphrey.

A recent project was to make clothes, in miniature, for five-year-old Rachel's three dolls. The nighties, dresses and trousers match all the clothes I have made for Rachel herself. I gave them to her as a Christmas present, in a baby-pink suitcase (from Schwartz in New York), all with matching hairbands (material ruched on to elastic – the same idea as a 'caterpillar' tie-back). That little girl's face as she opened the suitcase was a picture; she will never know the amount of pleasure it gave me – let alone her.

When I got married, at twenty-three, I found myself with two houses: a mews house in London and a seventeenth-century farmhouse in Devon, neither of which had any curtains. So I was faced with a total of about thirty-two basically curtain-less windows. I guessed that curtain making must be easier than dressmaking, and it is – it *truly* is. You are dealing with a two-dimensional object that doesn't move, as opposed to a three-dimensional object of complex shape.

I never found any courses or books that would teach me what I wanted to know, so it was trial and error and serious hard work for a while. I remember lying on a rug on the lawn at Beaulieu in Hampshire, and asking my aunt how to make a French pleat. (I'd only used dreadful tape before, and to say its pleats looked weak, tacky, and amateurish is an understatement.

They are just ghastly.) My aunt took hold of the edge of the rug and pinched 12cm (5in) together with one hand and then formed three pleats with the other. I soon realised how easily this professional look – and others – could be achieved.

One thing led to another. Friends started to request curtains and then the business snowballed. I worked in my bedroom in our tiny Kensington house on a piece of hardboard propped up between two other smaller tables. Gradually, I discovered various outworkers.

When our first baby was expected we moved to a gorgeous Victorian house in Clapham where I had a field day creating sensational window treatments. Meanwhile, the curtain-making business had become huge and hard to run: too many clients, too many outworkers to supervise and supply (trying to remember who needed which weight and width of interlining, which type of heading tape and hook, or which bolt of chintz and its contrast). Also, outworkers fell ill, or suddenly decided to go away for a month, and I was left stranded, with clients desperate for their drawing room or dining room to be finished before some grand party, or whatever. It was utterly exhausting.

Occasionally, I also had an impossible client: the type who gave you sleepless nights, tied your stomach in knots and made you want to throw the whole thing in for ever. I learned never to be put off, to take the rough with the smooth, and how to forget the bad clients pretty quickly and just enjoy the good ones.

I then had a fantastic break. I was asked to lecture for an organisation on window treatments. My husband built me a brilliant, free-standing mock window, complete with pelmet board, rail, pulley system and brass window furniture. I never looked back. I slowed down the curtain business just to very special jobs, and went on to lecture privately or for design centres all over Britain and America.

Having completed a teaching degree at Lady Spencer Churchill, Oxford, and spent four years teaching at Dulwich Prep, there is nothing I love more than teaching adults who are really eager to learn. It is enormous fun and highly satisfying revealing all the magic of the trade secrets, and lovely to see them going home at the end of the day, thrilled and confident about the subject.

Then I was approached to write a book or two. My first was *The Complete Book of Curtains and Drapes*; this is the second.

At this point I must say that I owe all my inspiration to my mother, who brought us up very lovingly. She stimulated and encouraged me in such a wonderful way that I have always wanted to create things, and take great pride in their results.

I do like cooking, but unfortunately it is messy, you have to clear up afterwards, and there are two big disadvantages: your creation totally disappears with great rapidity, and everyone is hungry again the next day. A beautiful bedroom, on the other hand, looks sensational for years and years, and a little smocked dress looks gorgeous for three generations. You can see why I prefer sewing.

Whether in recession or boom, it is still possible to live in real style, with all the comfort and elegance which one could ever wish for – on a very small budget. Making things for yourself is always possible for every furnishing situation. The only expense is the cost of the materials. The huge labour costs are free because you have done it yourself. What a joy!

It is, of course, all a question of time. Producing beautiful soft furnishings for your home is obviously time consuming, but it is deeply satisfying. The creative aspect is unbeatable. If you want something enough in life, you will always make time for it. Then, when you achieve it, the satisfaction is so huge – in this case, literally every time you walk into your bedroom – that it is worth every minute of careful designing, cutting, sewing, hanging and dressing.

The interior design of your bedroom seriously and rather honestly reflects you, the person (or people) who live in it. Its very personal nature means that you will probably want to get it as 'right', and comfortable, as possible. It should have all the elegance and comfort that one consciously creates for a drawing room, but it should reflect added qualities of prettiness, peace and a degree of reticence. Beautiful bedroom soft furnishing makes you want to stay in the bedroom. The opposite is merely depressing and unwelcoming.

This book shows you absolutely everything you need to know to create a glorious bedroom, from tips on style to meticulous step-by-step instructions. It will enable you to successfully achieve the look you want – and I hope you enjoy it for many years to come.

Lady Caroline Wrey

1

THE PERFECT
BEDROOM

An elegant bedroom is a joy to live in, and making the furnishings yourself gives pleasure and satisfaction for years. Creating the perfect look is easy once you are aware of the basic principles of design, and select your material carefully. In this chapter I guide you through my Seven-prong Plan of design using a particular bedroom as an example, and discuss the various types of furnishing materials available.

THE SEVEN-PRONG PLAN

When designing the furnishings in your bedroom, it is essential to consider all the following points:

1 Material choice
2 Direction of window
3 Light obstruction and view
4 Period of house
5 Occupant(s)/purpose of room
6 Trimmings
7 Overall style

This is what I call my Seven-prong Plan, and I always evaluate all these aspects when deciding how to furnish a room.

1 Material choice

Remember that you will be choosing something that you have to live with for a long time. You will see it every morning as you wake up, and every night as you go to sleep. When choosing material, unroll a length and assess it from a distance – as you will in the room. It might even be worth buying a metre or yard to take home and consider in the bedroom itself.

In this case, the predominant material is a particularly pretty yellow – so easy to live with. Yellow is a sunshine colour, and this cannot fail to brighten up a grey day. Yellow and blue are a beautiful combination, giving an atmosphere of happiness. There is such a quantity of it in this room that the impact is tremendous.

The other materials have been chosen with great care to tone in with and complement the main material. The overall effect is both interesting and completely harmonious.

2 Direction of window

Depending where you live in the world, there will be 'dark' directions and light directions. For example, in the Northern Hemisphere south and west receive more and stronger light, and north and east receive less. Therefore, you may wish to use warmer colours for less well-lit situations, whereas cooler colours should be considered where there is stronger light.

This window is probably west facing, which makes the choice of yellow material appropriate, since the room would be naturally deprived of morning sun. The lovely yellow would do a good job in brightening the room in the morning.

The light in a room may also affect your choice of material: chintz reflects light better than linen, for example.

3 Light obstruction and view

Being a bedroom on an upper floor, there is no light obstruction. The pelmet has been kept fairly short, to allow for maximum light, and sheers have not been used – obviously privacy is not a particular problem.

4 Period of house

There are no specific period features to influence design here. The room has reasonable height and space, but in order to hang a pelmet and the half tester in perfect proportion, there is very little ceiling clearance.

Very grand details such as swags and tails and half testers do not work in a modern, low-ceilinged house; similarly modern, bold fabrics would look out of place in a Georgian house.

5 Occupants of room

The furnishings here are pretty, peaceful and reticent. In terms of fullness and detail they are not overdone, yet the effect is supremely elegant. However, some people – especially men – might prefer a plainer environment. And for children, who study, play or relax more in their bedrooms, the functional requirements of the room should be borne in mind (see Children's Bedrooms, page 116).

6 Trimmings

There are many different blues that could have been chosen to use as a contrast in this room, but this deep navy blue is wonderful. The contrast along the gently curving lower edge perfectly accentuates the essential shape of the pelmet and the half tester. This is aided by the knotted swagging rope, which also adds depth and a three-dimensional quality to what would otherwise have been a very simple pelmet. Repeating this blue in piping on the seat, headboard and bedcover pulls together all the furnishings in the room.

The curtain tie-backs have been kept very simple, so as not to distract attention from the view through the window.

7 Overall style of room

The creator of this bedroom obviously decided to create a graceful and harmonious setting.

The most obvious balance is between the pelmets of the window and the half tester. But also the bedcover, valance, seat, dressing and round table covers, lamps, walls and floor covering all work beautifully together. The pelmets are not very full, but they are perfectly contrasted by the gathered bed valance and dressing table. Even the pattern on the carpet ties in with the trellis detail on the radiator casing.

Your final design

If you take into account all the aspects of the Seven-prong Plan, you cannot help but create a delightful and rewarding bedroom.

An elegant and delightful bedroom, making the most of warm yellow with the dark blue as a subtle balance. Each of the materials has been chosen with care to provide variety, yet combine harmoniously. Note how, by using the same design of pelmet, the window and the half tester tie in with each other.

MATERIAL CHOICES

When I think of all the hugely varying bedrooms I have slept in over the years, beautiful images of pretty chintzes filter through my mind. I have memories of waking up, as a child, in my pretty pink bedroom with the sun coming through gorgeous chintz curtains. They were utterly charming: yellow hammer birds flitting through apple blossom in full leaf. The background was just off white (such a soft colour) and my mother ad had the curtains made with a pink lining, so that when the light was behind it the background turned pink, as did the rest of the room. My mother made the box-pleated bed valance in matching chintz, and the bedcover, quite rightly, was white, as was the wicker headboard. The window pelmet [valance] was made on hard buckram with a scalloped lower edge,

which was fashionable at the time. The only disaster, as I recall, was when I attempted to give as many yellow birds as I could reach an extra specially big eye and smiley mouth with my fat, brown felt-tip pen. (I was five years old!)

In my current bedroom we now have curtains made from the most beautiful chintz. It is modern but refreshing and inspiring to look at: a white background with different sized tulips in pink and yellow, all accompanied by a peaceful green for the leaves and stalks. The pelmet heading is diamond smocked, outlined in a matching green silk skein.

During the year we stay in lovely country houses, at shooting house parties in the winter or fun weekends in the summer. I am always particularly aware of all the soft furnishing details in our bedroom, let alone the rest of the house (but, may I add, the

A peaceful and well-co-ordinated bedroom, and a good example of how no less than seven different materials can blend together beautifully.

company, food and general activities are of vital importance too!). There is no doubt that the bedroom themes of beautiful chinoiserie, peaceful toile de Jouy or pretty chintzes all add to a lovely welcoming feeling and desire to return to that particular house.

There is an enormous variety of fabrics from which to choose for furnishings. The following are best suited to bedrooms.

Floral chintzes

This is a printed cotton which is then glazed on one side to enhance its look. It originated in India and became highly popular in the eighteenth and early nineteenth centuries. The

This pretty room uses three different types of chintz to good effect – all held together by the use of the same colour in contrast piping.

original designs were floral, as are many still: think of all the sprigs, garlands and bouquets of flowers. Chintz is very evocative of the country and conjures up dreamy perennials and annuals you find growing in a herbaceous border, for example. I always think it is particularly fitting to use chintzes in the city, to remind you of lovely country houses.

It is therefore less necessary to use floral chintzes in the country since the view and the world outside is the real thing. This is when I might veer towards plainer designs, stripes or checks. Yet floral chintzes are often perfect for bedrooms: so timeless, romantic and easy to live with. They are also easy to design with, balancing them with plain silks or linens.

Plain chintzes

As many material manufacturers produce large ranges of plain chintzes, it is easy to pick just the right colour to match or complement a patterned material – a decision that is probably the final 'icing on the cake' in terms of design. It is the correct colour of plain chintz (on the bed valance or corona lining, or on a little chair, perhaps) that perfectly balances the room. Plain chintz can be used for tiny details, such as the colour of the buttons on a headboard, that contribute hugely to 'pulling together' the colour scheme of the entire room.

Unglazed cottons

There is a great deal of cotton material on the market, both old and new. A matt as opposed to a glazed look is equally beautiful in a bedroom, especially when you possibly use this fabric on the walls as well.

Toile de Jouy

This material, originally Indian, but copied by the Europeans, has been printed outside Paris at Jouy for over 200 years. Engraved designs are printed onto an unglazed, off-white cotton, usually in reds, blues and greens and mauves. A whole room done in this wonderfully simple stuff has a dramatic effect.

I love all the toiles you can buy – whether they are pastoral scenes, chinoiserie, Spanish galleons or hot air balloons. They all look wonderful in their simple colours. The curtains in one of my grandmother's guest rooms are made out of a lovely subtle mauve toile with a pastoral scene, and the same material is stretched over one of the four walls – the one opposite the window. It looks extremely stylish, even though the decoration is forty years old. I have also used toile de Jouy in guest rooms in Provence; it is just perfect for that immensely hot, beautiful and peaceful part of the world.

Silks

In bedrooms, silks are gorgeous and very grand. Depending on the density or quality of the silk, you may often want to use thick bump for interlining (see page 12) instead of medium, since this will give the stuff real body and arrest the speed of fading caused by the sun's ultraviolet rays. However, do not use heavy bump in a silk pelmet – use the medium interlining.

Voiles and muslins

There are endless beautiful materials on the market, which are deliberately produced to hang as sheer curtains. I would highly recommend cotton laces. Don't even consider synthetic sheer materials; they look cheap, no matter how you use them.

The translucent quality of this type of fabric adds an interesting extra dimension to any window treatment. Not only do the heavy lace-type weaves in white or off-white look brilliant but thin white or cream silks (unlined) look fabulous. I sometimes put a white silk, unlined, pair of curtains in a master bedroom, on a separate rail system from the main set of curtains, set right back against the window (see page 77). This gives total privacy but does not lose any light. You can wash or clean these curtains frequently with no trouble. Equally, lace or voile sheers are easy to look after.

Sheers in the form of an Austrian blind are also effective in bedrooms, and even more when one of those dreaded architects (who know nothing about window treatments) have inevitably decided that the only place in the entire room to put a radiator is under the window – a nightmare.

Linens

These are probably a little heavy for bedroom curtaining but certainly perfect for those small bits of furniture like chairs, *chaise longues*, stools or a headboard. Whatever the use, do bear in mind that linen creases very easily.

Damasks

Damask was originally made in Damascus in the fourteenth century. It is a figured material in which a matt design is woven into a satin weave, usually in the shape of flowers, fruit or figures. Damasks were originally produced in silk, but later also in linen and cotton. There is a highly successful modern interpretation of damask which is a printed, as opposed to woven, version of the designs.

Damasks look gorgeous in bedrooms. In the eighteenth and nineteenth centuries four-poster beds were often dressed in lovely, thick, richly coloured damasks. In freezing cold houses in that era, it would have been vital to be able to draw one's bed curtains around four-posters for warmth.

LININGS AND INTERLININGS

These are needed for most bedroom furnishings for the best effect to be achieved. Traditional methods of lining and interlining have never been surpassed for creating a rich depth, and producing lovely folds which hang beautifully. Thick curtains will look sumptuous and, when drawn, will flow with a fluid movement.

Plain linings

For lining material, a pure cotton sateen is preferred and is the most widely available curtain lining on the market. It usually comes either 120cm (48in) or 137cm (54in) wide. It is worth buying the wider lining. Although it is slightly more expensive per metre (yard) than narrower lining, you will probably find that your chosen material is nearer to 137cm (54in) wide than 120cm (48in). It will therefore save you the effort of joining panels in the narrower width in order to make it up to the correct finished width for the outer material.

Sateen lining comes in a wide range of colours; however, neutral colours – white, ivory, ecru and beige – are the ones most commonly used. Ivory is the best colour to use for most curtains and pelmets. It is much more pleasing to the eye than a stark, cold white; it does not look as dirty as white will after a few years of hanging, and it will also not show discolouration from exposure to light in the way white does.

Beige lining is rarely recommended. It is very dark and therefore discolours easily from the light. It would also show through any white-background chintzes and spoil their appearance.

Coloured linings

Although coloured linings look very pretty when you see them on a bolt of material, they are not such a good idea for curtains because their dyes are not strong. The sun is capable of draining the colour out of a curtain lining in a few years, especially if it is facing the south or west. This is terribly disappointing after going to all the effort and expense involved in curtain making. If you are determined to have a coloured curtain lining, you would do better to choose a very cheap, thin, plain chintz. The dyes in these chintzes are relatively colourfast.

Where coloured linings are deliberately used, as for the inside of a corona curtain a coloured chintz is used as it looks of much better quality.

If you are thinking of using a coloured lining for a bedroom curtain in order to keep the morning sun out, why not order a coloured roller blind instead?

Synthetic linings

It is best to avoid using synthetic linings, as they have no redeeming features. There are certain synthetic linings that are sold as a single alternative to the double combination of both lining and interlining. But these fabrics are solid and graceless. I would strongly advise you not to use them.

Lightweight interlining

Lightweight interlining, or 'domette' (see Glossary on page 123 for a suggested American equivalent), is essential in caught-up pelmets (see page 92), since they must retain a 'light' look.

I have only ever used lightweight interlining in curtains when I have wanted them to look very light and airy. This is usually when designing curtains to be used in a country with a hot climate.

Medium-weight interlining

Medium-weight interlining is the best for almost all curtain materials. Also called 'bump' (see Glossary on page 123 for American equivalent), it is a multi-purpose, thick, furry cotton fabric. It is used for curtains, pelmets and bedcovers.

Bump has wonderful qualities that I never tire of praising. It has a soft yet firm body that makes your furnishings look heavy, thick and lavish. It also protects the print of curtain material from the sun, insulates the room beautifully, and helps the fluid movement of the curtains as they are drawn backwards and forwards across the window.

In addition, medium-weight interlining is incredibly easy to work with. It frays very little and is very manageable when being moved, reacting much like a soft, light, firm woolly blanket. But *beware of your clothes* – bump will leave a dreadful white fluff on everything, which is a special disaster on navy blue and on black!

Heavy interlining

I rarely use heavy interlining, except in three specific situations. Firstly when designing curtains that need to look very, very thick and lavish, I will use heavy interlining as a special luxury. Secondly, most silks are fairly thin and will need that extra body that a heavy bump will give. And thirdly, certain unglazed cottons will require a heavier interlining because they tend to crease more easily than chintz.

CLEANING

All types of soft furnishings will need cleaning at some stage during their life. Gently vacuum-clean them on a gentle setting with a soft upholstery attachment.

Never wash soft furnishings. Mostly, it will wreck them irredeemably. Any attempt to wash interlining will be a complete disaster, as it is so loosely woven. Washing chintz removes its glaze, which can never be replaced.

Very dirty materials may have to be dry-cleaned, but this should be done by someone who is very experienced in this field and can treat the interlining with the greatest respect. (See suppliers, page 124.)

A wonderfully masculine room where the plain, strong colours create a rich but cosy atmosphere – all offset by the white bed linen.

2

BASIC TECHNIQUES

Having the correct tools, and mastering certain simple techniques, will make the entire procedure of making soft furnishings an easy task, allowing you to work fast and efficiently. This chapter explains about tools, cutting materials, joining, pattern-matching and trimmings, all of which will help you achieve a professional result.

BASIC EQUIPMENT

You will see that the equipment listed below is minimal. Although a professional sewer may have a larger work space and larger tables to work on, the tools that he or she uses are the same as those listed below.

Aside from the obvious sewing machine and iron, they include:
– Two pairs of table clamps
– A large trestle table
– A 2m (6ft) folding ruler
– A 15cm (6in) transparent plastic ruler
– A soft tape measure
– Sewing scissors and pinking shears
– A pocket calculator
– A manual staple gun (for pelmets, coronas, headboards or half testers)
– An aluminium stepladder
– Extra-long pins and needles.

Table clamps

Two pairs of extra-strong table clamps are probably more important than any of the other tools listed. They enable you to deal with large amounts of material on a relatively small table.

The clamps hold the material very firmly in place, never allowing it to move while you are cutting, sewing or pinning long lengths of fabric. They also enable you to manoeuvre into place interlining, lining or fusible buckram while your fabric remains still. The difference between sewing stretched and clamped fabric and loose fabric is extraordinary. The clamps will make the sewing both quicker and easier, and your hand stitches will automatically become more regular and even in tension. For me, using clamps is like having another person always helping you – but silently!

The type of clamp pictured has no jagged edges and will never mark your material in any way, nor will it damage any ordinary hardwood table. However, it is not advisable to risk using any sort of clamp on a valuable antique table.

Although these clamps are not always easy to find, they are well worth the search. Professional photographic equipment shops may sometimes stock them. (Also see the list of suppliers on page 124.)

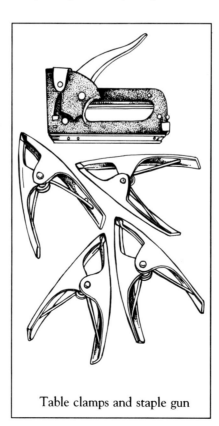

Table clamps and staple gun

Trestle table

You must never try to work on the floor. It is both uncomfortable and impractical. Physically it is terribly bad for your back and your circulation. In addition, working on the floor does not allow the use of the invaluable table clamps.

A sturdy trestle table measuring approximately 1.80m by 70cm (6ft by 2ft 3in) is the minimum-sized table you could successfully work on when sewing fairly wide curtain (or bedcover) panels, such as a finished flat width of 3m (9ft 10in). Obviously, however, the bigger the table is, the better it is for you. The table must also have a wide enough lip, not too thick, to accommodate the table clamps.

As already mentioned, it is not advisable to use an antique table for sewing. Aside from being marked by clamps, it could be scratched by the needle when interlocking the interlining to fabric, or other hand sewing.

You must always sit while you work. If you stand you will end up bending over your work, which is a strain on your back. Simply move your chair around the table to the side you are working on at the time.

Folding ruler

A wooden folding ruler 2m (6ft) long is an absolute necessity for making soft furnishings. A ruler with metric measurements on one side and inches

Once basic techniques – such as making frills, piping and pattern matching – have been mastered, it is easy to create a wealth of different furnishings for your bedroom.

and feet on the other is especially useful for those who are just getting to grips with the metric system. (Remember, though, to choose one system and *stick to it*; trying to mix the two is a recipe for disaster.) This type of ruler is brilliant, as it enables you to measure any curtain drop up to about 4m (13ft) without having to use a ladder. This is because it is totally rigid, like a yardstick, and can easily be held up the side of a window architrave to measure it.

A long folding ruler is also used when measuring the diameter and drop of round tables; the dimensions of a bed base for a valance; and the height of coronas and headboards. Using a rigid measuring instrument for these is much easier and quicker than using a soft tape measure. (See list of suppliers, page 124.)

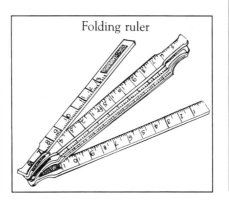

Folding ruler

Transparent plastic ruler
A transparent plastic ruler 15cm (6in) long is a very efficient little item to use for measuring while sewing, and is often more practical than a soft tape measure. Being small and flat, it rarely slips on to the floor, unlike a tape measure. Also, you can see through it, as you gently turn back hems to their correct width. On an ironing board especially, a little ruler is the only thing to use if you want to work fast and efficiently.

Soft tape measure
I rarely use a soft tape measure. But there are several situations when it must be substituted for your long rigid ruler: when you need to measure around the girth of a curtain to estimate the size of the tie-back; when measuring a curved bay window; and measuring up for a bedcover.

Scissors and pinking shears
It may be obvious that you must always use a very good pair of large sewing scissors to make cutting-out easier, but I feel that this point is worth reiterating. Bad scissors are frustrating and will slow you down considerably; for example, when you are trying to cut interlining away from the corners of your curtains.

Good scissors are not expensive, but it is essential to hide them from the rest of the family so that they are used for cutting material and nothing else. Paper will blunt them immediately.

Pinking shears are needed for edges that will be turned to the wrong side but not doubled under, such as on certain handmade frills (see pages 18–21).

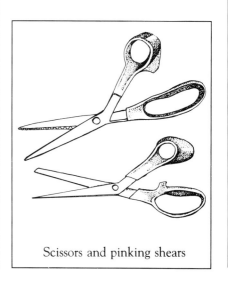

Scissors and pinking shears

Pocket calculator

There is no point in doing multiplication and division yourself, when a calculator will do it for you in a fraction of a second. This small piece of equipment makes calculating fabric quantities, pattern repeats, and sizes and positions of goblet pleats quick and painless.

Staple gun

You can buy a manual staple gun in any do-it-yourself shop, and you will find it invaluable. This is primarily because it's the only way to attach Velcro, used for pelmets, coronas, Austrian blinds, and half testers.

You also need a staple gun to cover a headboard.

Stepladder

A stepladder will obviously be needed to hang most curtains, fix pelmets and arrange a corona. An average-sized aluminium stepladder will be tall enough if the top of your window or ceiling (for a corona) is up to 3m (10ft) from the floor. A window (or ceiling) taller than this will require a wooden ladder. Although a wooden ladder will generally do, I much prefer an aluminium one because it is so light and easy to move around.

Stepladder

Extra-long pins and needles

Pins and needles may be a normal part of sewing equipment, but for furnishings it is important to use extra-long pins and needles preferably with round glass or plastic ends.

The type of needles required for the long stitches used in curtain making are *long darners*. You will waste a lot of time and effort trying to use shorter needles or pins.

CUTTING FABRICS

When you have purchased your material, lining and interlining (see pages 10–12), you can now proceed to create your bedroom furnishings.

To prepare for cutting your fabrics, pull your work table out into the room so that you can easily walk around it. Make sure that the floor is very clean around the table, as the lengths of fabric will often need to hang down on the floor. And last, have all the necessary tools close to hand.

Meaning of drop and width

These two words mean exactly the same thing, even though one seems to suggest something vertical and the other something horizontal. I tend to think, and talk, far more about widths than drops. So when I am referring to the number of widths in a curtain, I mean the number of lengths of material cut off the bolt of material and then machine stitched together to make up one curtain. This applies to all other furnishings as well. For example, with bed valances, the number of widths needed for a valance skirt refers to the number of pieces, cut to a certain length, needed to make up the long strip which goes around the sides of the bed.

Cutting material

1 Check your calculations one last time to make sure that the *cutting length* of each width of material is correct, and check that you have enough fabric.

2 Before measuring the first width, or drop, check that the grain of the material is straight along the starting edge. To do this, unfold the material so that the starting edge is aligned with one end of the table and one selvedge is aligned with the edge of the length of the table. With the selvedge aligned

Straightening a crooked edge

with the table in this way you can use the right-angle corner at the end of the table to straighten the end of the material. Clamp the material to the table before cutting to hold it in place (see *Table clamps* page 14). Then, resting the scissors along the edge of the table as you cut, trim the top of the material to straighten it.

3 With the starting edge still level with one end of the table, unroll the material the whole length of the table and clamp it in place, keeping one selvedge aligned with the edge of the table. Using the unfolded 2m (6ft) folding ruler, measure down along the selvedge as far as your table will allow and, with a pencil, mark the selvedge. Then unclamp and unroll more material, moving it on to the table. Again measure down along the selvedge until the total cutting length is reached, and mark the selvedge. Unclamp, move back to the beginning of the material and measure down the other selvedge in the same way.

4 In order to mark the cutting line gently turn the material 90 degrees so that the selvedges are running at a right angle to the length of the table and both selvedges are resting on it. Put your long ruler across the table and join up the two final marks on the selvedges. Draw a line across the material, running the pencil along the ruler. (If you are worried about marking the material you can use a disappearing marker or pins – but if you have carefully checked your cutting length calculations and fabric amount, you will not be running any risk.) Cut

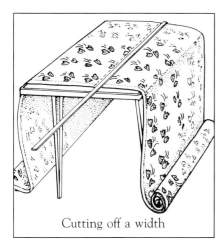

Cutting off a width

along the line using straight-edged scissors.

5 You must now cut any remaining widths. Unroll another quantity of material and clamp in the same way as for the first width. If you are using patterned material take the first width you have already cut, and match its pattern by lining it up temporarily with the uncut material. Don't bother to clamp or pin; you are merely checking where to cut the next width. (See diagram below of pattern-matching.) Make a mark on the selvedge to indicate where the next length of fabric will begin. Measure the distance from the mark just made to the top of the material, so that you can now mark the opposite selvedge the same distance from the top. Join up the two

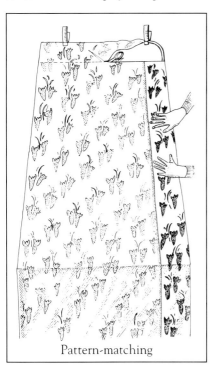

Pattern-matching

marks as you did for the lower edge of the first width. This removes any excess of pattern repeat, so that the pattern will match at the seams. You are now ready to cut the second width. Repeat the same process followed when cutting the first width. Cut as many widths as required in the same way, pattern-matching each width.

6 After all of the necessary widths of material have been cut, they should be stored with care while any lining and interlining widths needed are cut. Roll the widths you will not be using right away back on to the bolt to avoid creasing them. This is not easy, and if possible you should get the help of another person, who can guide the material back on to the bolt as you turn it. They may spiral off a little at one end, but do not worry. So long as the widths are rolled up in this manner they will never crease.

Creases, especially in chintz, are very hard to get rid of without the use of a steam iron. (Always iron the material from the wrong side, since the steam would damage the glaze of the chintz, and you can *never* re-glaze it.)

Selvedges

Selvedges are rarely cut off on any material. On some fabrics, however, there may be a situation when the writing on the selvedge is rather prominent. And if the background of the print is white, then it is important that the writing does not show through, so it has to be cut off. This particularly applies to curtains, where light shines through. The selvedge may also cause a problem if it is rather tight, which sometimes happens with linen. In this case it is sufficient to snip the selvedge intermittently to ease it.

JOINING THE WIDTHS

Before machine stitching the material widths together, you must pin the seam edges together. If the fabric is plain and does not require pattern-matching, you can simply place the edges together with right sides facing, pin and machine stitch. If your material is a print, however, it must be pattern-matched while pinning.

Pattern-joining material
1 Clamp the first width of material to the table, right side up, with the selvedge running along the very edge of the length of the table and the top of the material at one end.

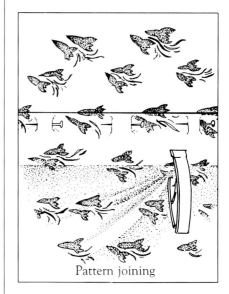

Pattern joining

2 Now take the second width and line up its selvedge (also right side up) with the first width on the table so that the pattern matches. Turn under the selvedge of the second width, and pin it to the clamped width, matching the pattern carefully. Pin the two pieces together along the length of the table, inserting the pins vertically along the turned-under selvedge and placing them about 21cm (8in) apart.

3 Before moving the fabric along to pin the rest of the seam, run the closed blades of your scissors along the pinned seam. By doing this you will make a permanent, firm crease along the fold line – a quick and effective way without using a hot iron. The reason for the hard crease will become apparent in a moment. Unclamp the material, then pin and crease the rest of the seam in the same way.

4 Then, beginning at the top of the material width again, bring the second width over on top of the first width, so that the right sides of the pieces are together. Now insert a pin horizontally across the sharp fold line made in step 3, in each space between the vertical pins (see above). Do this along the entire length of the fabric.

5 After all of the horizontal pins are in place, remove the first lot of vertical pins.

6 You are now ready to machine stitch the two widths accurately down the sharp fold line. Any additional widths are pinned and sewn in the same way.

Machine stitching

Before seaming the material, test your sewing machine on a scrap of fabric. If there is a problem sewing it, continue experimenting on remnants of the material until the tension and size of your stitches (fairly large) are correct. This is much more satisfactory than having to unpick errors in the real thing.

Always use matching thread and a fairly strong needle – size 90/14 will do for most jobs and is also strong enough for fusible buckram.

Having machine stitched the widths together, take them to the ironing board. Then with the right sides of the fabric together and the seams still unopened, press on the wrong side along the stitches to embed them. After this, lay the material right side down and press the seams open and flat. You will now have a perfect pattern join.

Joining lining widths

Lining widths do not need to be pattern-joined, so they should be simply pinned right sides together and machine stitched 1.5cm (½in) from the edge, using a matching thread. After machine stitching, press the seams to embed the stitches. Then press the seams open and flat in the same way as the main material seams (see above).

Joining interlining widths

Interlining for bedcovers and curtains are joined in a different way from the lining and main materials. Overlap the widths, 1.5cm (½in), one on top of the other, and machine stitch them together, using a large zigzag stitch, down the middle of the overlapped fabric. This method minimises the bulk.

FRILLS

Frills are a component of design that can give an extra dimension to your furnishings. Instructions are given here for all the basic frills that you might wish to add to a valance, table cover, curtain or pelmet.

Making frills is incredibly popular in the curtain classes I give. The process seems to give enjoyment because it is so quickly learned and because the resulting frills are so professional-looking and effective; and because they cost virtually nothing, especially when compared to commercially produced fringes, etc.

Set-on or inset

A frill can be added to a main item such as a curtain or pelmet in two ways. It can be *inset*: stitched into a seam so that its raw edge is sandwiched between the main material and lining; or *set-on* an already hemmed edge, when both the frill's edges are turned back (see Frontispiece).

Frills and pelmet drop

I always include handmade frills in the total finished drop of a pelmet, as they are a solid edge. Bullions, however, I tend to add on as an extra to the finished length of the drop, because a lot of light comes through them.

Choosing materials

The easiest material to use for frills is chintz, because it is so easy to fold and gather. But you should always match your frill to your main material, using chintz to edge chintz, silk to edge silk and so on. If your main fabric is a print, use either the same print or a rich solid colour for the frill.

Always use matching thread when machine stitching your frills.

Cutting and joining

Frill pieces should always be cut on the straight grain of the material. This may be the crosswise grain (selvedge to selvedge) or the lengthwise grain (parallel to the selvedge).

If the frill material is a print, do not attempt to match the pattern when joining seams. It is totally unnecessary. Over such a short width a mismatch will never be noticed – especially once the strip is gathered or pleated.

Machine-gathered frill

As a trimming, the handmade machine-gathered frill has a soft and subtle character.

You will see that the gathering is done by hand at the same time the strip of material is fed through the machine. The technique used in dressmaking of pulling long, loose machine stitches is not possible when making long lengths of trimming. Evening up the gathers would be very time-consuming and the threads would inevitably break at some point while being pulled over the long lengths needed for the frills.

Gathering while machine stitching is an easy technique to pick up and needs only a little practice on scraps of material.

Making the frill

1 For a finished frill 6cm (2¼in) deep, you would cut strips of material 15cm

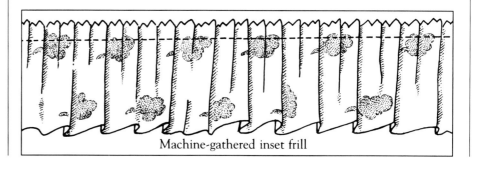

Machine-gathered inset frill

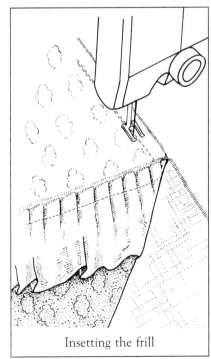

Both ways of adding a frill can be seen here: the curtains are completed with a double, set-on frill using both the main material and the pink contrast; while the pillow shams on the bed have a more subtle inset frill.

Making a gathered frill

(6in) wide. This will allow for a 1.5cm (½in) final seam allowance along the top of the doubled-over material. Cut enough strips for the entire frill, allowing 2½ times the finished edge to be frilled.

2 Join all the strips together end to end with 1.5cm (½in) seams, and press the seams open. Remember that it is totally unnecessary to pattern-match.

3 Fold the joined strip in half lengthwise with wrong sides and raw edges together. Do not press the fold yet, and do not pin.

4 Machine gather along the strip by making little tucks in the material continuously, one after another, as the material is fed through the machine. The stitches should run alongside (and just below) the stitches along the top of the frill. The trick in gathering is to use your two middle fingers to feed the material, using

Insetting the frill

more pressure on the right hand, which is on the seam allowance. It is essential, especially with chintz, to lick your two fingers occasionally so that they grip. Stop and start the machine continually, as you make the little tucks (see above). *Do not press a machine-gathered frill after gathering.*

5 Measure the finished frill to ensure that the frill is long enough for its purpose (it can be trimmed to fit).

6 If you are insetting the frill, now machine stitch the lining to the main material, right sides together, so that the frill is sandwiched between the two fabrics. With the main material facing, stitch along the previous stitches but 1.5cm (½in) from the edge (see diagram above). Open and press.

Machine-pleated frill

Machine pleating has a far stronger, heavier and more tailored character than machine gathering. Like machine gathering, however, this frill is quick and easy to make after a little practice on scraps of fabric.

As for machine-gathered frills, I recommend a 6cm (2¼in)-deep finished frill for pelmets with a drop from 30cm to 45cm (12in to 18in).

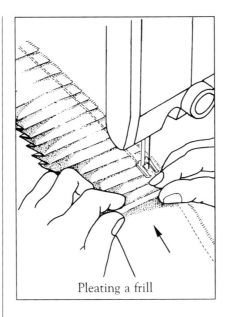

Pleating a frill

3 Having machine pleated the frill, you must now *iron the pleats in* to make them look sharp and organized.

4 Follow steps 5 and 6 of the machine-gathered frill to sew the frill to the lower edge of the pelmet.

Permanently pleated inset frill

The permanently pleated frill is one of my favourite methods of trimming pelmets. To me, it is the ultimate in elegance.

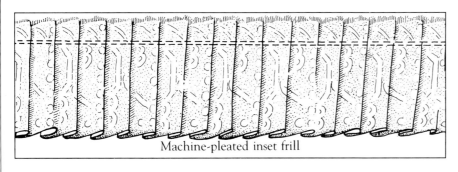

Machine-pleated inset frill

Making the frill

1 Cut and prepare the strips as for a machine-gathered frill, steps 1–3, but when cutting the strips, allow 3 times around what you want to frill, as opposed to 2½.

2 Follow step 4 of the machine-gathered frill, but instead of making little tucks, make pleats about 1cm (½in) deep continuously, one after another, along the folded strip. There is no need to measure each pleat; just fold them under each time, using your eye as the guide to width (see below).

To make this frill you must hem long strips of fabric and send them off to a commercial pleater (see list of suppliers on page 124) for permanent pleating. I would recommend that you ask for a 4mm (⅛in) pleating, which is usually the narrowest available and the most elegant. This narrow pleating is highly suitable for bedrooms. If you want a frill with a stronger and bolder presence, ask for 8mm (¼in) pleating.

First find out from the pleating company how long the flat frill strips should be. They will generally work

with strips no longer than 10m (11yd). So if your finished pelmet will be longer than about 3m (3¼yd) you may need to prepare more than one strip and sew them together after pleating.

The instructions given are for a finished inset frill of 6cm (2¼in), but of course you can create deeper frills, if necessary.

Making the frill

1 For a finished frill 6cm (2¼in) deep, cut strips of material 9cm (3½in) wide, *using pinking shears.* This will allow for a 1.5cm (½in) final seam allowance along the top for setting in and 1.5cm (½in) along the bottom for turning up. Cut enough of these strips for the entire frill, allowing 3 times the finished pelmet length. Then join the strips end to end with 1.5cm (½in) seams, and press the seams open.

2 Fold back 1.5cm (½in) at one short end of one of the two strips, and machine stitch 8mm (¼in) from the folded edge. Then turn under 1.5cm (½in) all along the lower edge of the strip, and press, using a short clear plastic ruler to check the width. Using matching thread, machine stitch along the lower edge 8mm (¼in) from the folded edge. Press to embed the stitches.

3 Fold up the strip and send or take it to a commercial pleater for pleating, (see list of suppliers, page 124) specifying the width of pleat desired.

4 The fabric will be returned pleated and lightly stuck to a very thin paper. Unroll the frill, and, using paper-cutting scissors, cut roughly around the strip(s) without pulling off the paper. Machine stitch along the top of the frill 1cm (⅜in) from the raw edge, stitching through both fabric and paper. This will hold the top of the pleats in place.

5 Before setting the frill into the pelmet, as for steps 5 and 6 of the machine-gathered frill, gently tear away the thin paper. (Don't worry if bits get stuck and left in the seam allowance at the frill's top.)

Contrast-bound set-on frill

A machine-gathered or pleated frill can be bound on the top and bottom with a contrasting colour to create two parallel lines along the frill. It is possible to create a similar effect by binding only the lower edge of an inset frill and pipiing (U.S., 'cording') the lower edge of the pelmet, but this is a longer process.

Making the frill

1 For a finished frill 7cm (2¾in) deep, cut strips of the main material 7cm (2¾in) wide. Cut enough strips for the entire frill, allowing 2½ times the finished length for a gathered frill and 3 times for a pleated frill. Then join the strips as in step 2 of a machine-gathered frill.

2 For the contrasting binding, cut strips of contrasting material 4cm (1½in) wide, *using pinking shears*. Cut and then join enough strips to make two lengths of binding: one to bind the top edge of the frill and one to bind the bottom edge.

3 Place one binding strip along one edge of the main strip with right sides and two raw edges together. Machine stitch along the length of the strips 1cm (⅜in) from the raw edges. Then sew the second contrasting strip to the other edge in the same way. Before turning back the bindings, press the stitching to embed the stitches.

4 Lay the strip on the ironing board face up, and keeping the main strip flat, press back the bindings, pressing from the centre of the frill outwards. Then, using a clear plastic ruler to check width as you press, fold under the excess binding fabric to create a 1cm (⅜in) binding on the right side. Do this at both the top and bottom of the frill. Do not turn under the raw edge, as the pinked edge will be neat enough for the wrong side of the frill.

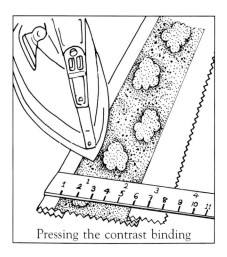

Pressing the contrast binding

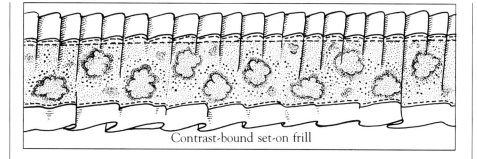

Contrast-bound set-on frill

5 With the right side of the frill facing upwards, topstitch along the binding, just to one side of it, on the main fabric (see below). To ensure that the stitching is hardly visible, use thread matching the main material, and stitch as close as possible to the binding. Do this on both top and bottom of frill. Press.

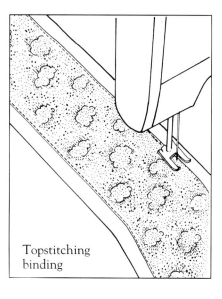

Topstitching binding

6 Folding under 1.3cm (½in) at the beginning, gather or pleat the bound frill as in step 4 of the machine-gathered frill, or pleat as in steps 2 and 3 of the machine-pleated frill, stitching 1.5cm (½in) from the top of the frill. There is now a little 'stand-up' along the top of the frill.

7 To attach the frill to the curtain, pelmet or table cover, machine stitch in the correct position, working over the gathering or pleating stitches, and cutting the frill to the correct length. Finish the end like the beginning.

RUCHING

This is a technique used for creating a gathered border or band, where a strip of material is gathered on both sides. For this you need to allow 3 times the length of the finished band.

The strip of material is machine gathered on each side, both times running it through the machine in the same direction. It is helpful to allow about 3cm (1¼in) seam allowance on the left-hand side to give your fingers something to hold on to, while guiding the strip through the machine.

PIPING

Many soft furnishing items have piped seams or piped frills as an added detail. Always pipe where directed – it gives a much more professional finish.

Piping strips are always cut on the bias or cross grain of the fabric. The strips of material are joined with diagonal seams, and then the piping cord is covered with the material, and machined with a zipper foot so you can stitch really close to the cord. (See steps 1 and 2, page 30.)

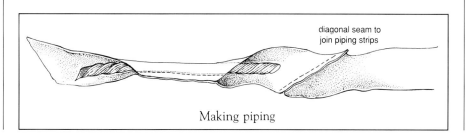

diagonal seam to join piping strips

Making piping

3

INSTANT ELEGANCE

If you would like your bed linens to tie in with the rest of your room, it is
probably best to make your own, as you are then not limited to purchasing ready-
made designs. The following projects give directions for quick, simple projects
that take only a little time and effort to make. Provided the material has been
chosen carefully, the effect in the room is instant: automatic elegance for your bed.

MATERIAL FOR BED LINENS

Many big department stores sell lovely printed or plain sheeting, which is just perfect for matching duvet and pillow covers. It is possible to buy cotton/polyester mixes, 100 per cent cotton, or even linen which, although expensive, is glorious to sleep in.

If your duvet cover and pillow are in total harmony with the rest of the room, then they will be a lovely feature in themselves that certainly do not need covering up by a bedcover.

PILLOW CASE

Finished size: 71cm × 47cm (28in × 18½in)
Material quantity: 50cm (20in) of 1.75m (5ft 9in) wide sheeting

French seams are used here, to give a neat and attractive finished pillow case.

1 Cut sheeting 1.68m (5ft 6in) long and 50cm (20in) wide. Press 4cm

(1½in) over, wrong sides together, at one of the short ends of the pillow case. Then press 4cm (1½in) more over again and machine stitch along the fold. Press.

2 Press 2cm (¾in) over, wrong sides together, at the other short end of the pillow case. Machine stitch along fold. Press.

3 Fold 16cm (6½in) down at this same end, wrong sides together. Machine stitch along the two side raw edges to hold material in place.

4 Fold pillow case so that wrong sides are together and the two ends are

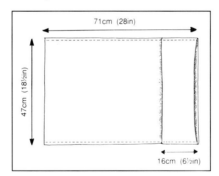

level. Machine stitch up the two long sides, along the raw edges, with ½cm (¼in) seam allowance.

5 To sew French seams, turn, wrong sides out, and press seams. Machine stitch along both long seams with a 1cm (⅜in) seam allowance. Press and turn back to right side out.

PILLOW SHAM

A pillow sham looks good either all in a plain white or pastel colour, or with a contrast, floral frill.

Finished size (inclusive of frill): 79cm × 55cm (31in × 22in)
Material quantity: Sham: 50cm (20in) × 1.75m (5ft 9in) sheeting
Frill: 30cm (12in) × 1.75m (5ft 9in)

1 Cut front sham 73cm × 49cm (29in × 19½in).

2 Cut two pieces for the back of the sham: 49cm × 42cm (19½in × 17in).

3 Cut frilling strips 6cm (2½in) wide to total 8.10m (9yd) in length (to measure 2½ times round the edge).

4 Join all frill strips together, and fold long strip in half, wrong sides together. Machine gather frilling (see pages 18–19).

5 Pin raw edges of filling around all four sides of front, right side of pillow sham, so that it faces into the middle. Machine stitch with a 1cm (⅜in) seam allowance.

6 Press 0.5cm (¼in) over on the right-hand long side of one back piece of the sham. Then fold over a further 0.5cm

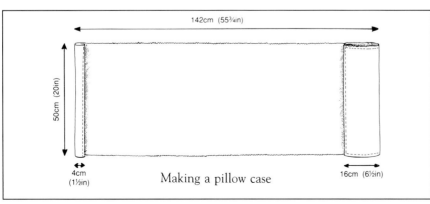

Making a pillow case

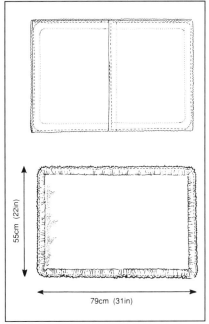

(¼in) and press. Machine stitch along the fold. Press. Repeat to the other piece of back but this time on the left-hand side.

7 Pin these two back pieces, right sides and all raw edges together, around all four sides of the front, frilled pillow sham. When you do so make sure that at the centre back, the two pieces overlap by 3cm (1¼in). Machine stitch around all four sides. Trim seam and oversew with a close zigzag stitch. Turn and press.

DUVET COVER

Finished size, standard double: 1.88m long × 1.35m wide (6ft 2in × 4ft 6in).
Material quantity: this slightly depends on the width of the sheeting

Crisp, white sheets and pillows and a simple bedcover co-ordinated with the rest of the room, create a plain, but instantly elegant effect.

you choose to buy but most likely for this size bed you will buy approx 1.75m (5ft 9in) wide sheeting. You will need 1.94m × 2 = 3.88m (6ft 5in × 2 = 4yd 1ft)

1 Cut 2 widths 1.94m (6ft 5in) long.

2 Press up 1cm (½in) along the short side of one end of the sheeting. Then press up 3cm (1¼in). Machine stitch along the edge of this fold and press. Repeat all this to the other cut of the sheeting.

3 Seam up the remaining three sides of the duvet cover. It is best to use the French seam method: it is the neatest

ABOVE *Simple pillows and pillow shams suit this delightfully minimalist four-poster bed.*

LEFT *Quick, simple projects such as pillow slips and a duvet cover, made in matching materials, can instantly create an elegant effect on the bed.*

and quickest way to achieve a good finish on these inside seams. So put the wrong sides together of the two pieces of sheeting (i.e. right sides out), with the three raw edges level. Machine around, 0.5cm (¼in) in from the edge.

4 Turn cover so it is wrong sides out. Press all seams carefully. Machine stitch around three sides with a 1cm (⅜in) seam allowance. Turn to right sides out and press seams.

5 15cm (6in) in from the side seam, at the foot end, put the 3cm (1¼in) turning on top of the other and pin. Machine across the turning. Secure stitches well. Repeat at the other side.

6 Mark out button holes, approx every 12cm (5in), all the way across the duvet opening. Buy appropriate 2cm (¾in) buttons and stitch your button holes along the turning.

CHAIR CUSHION

Finished size: 40cm × 40cm (16in × 16in), plus a piped, double-pleated frill of 2.5cm (1in)

The most important thing about cushion covers is that the filling, or pad, must be a little larger than the cover. This is so that the inside entirely holds the shape of the cushion, even when the cushion has been sat against. Therefore, for this cover you will need a pad 45cm (18in) square.

Material quantity: 75m (30in) of 1.40m (56in) wide. Plus 25cm (10in) 2cm (¾in)-wide Velcro.

1 Cut two pieces of material 44cm × 42cm (18in × 17in) wide.

2 Cut frilling strips 7cm (3in) wide to total 5m (5½yd). Join together and fold strip, wrong sides together. Make into a pleated frill (see page 20), then pipe frill (see page 21).

3 With raw edges together, pin pleated frill around four sides of

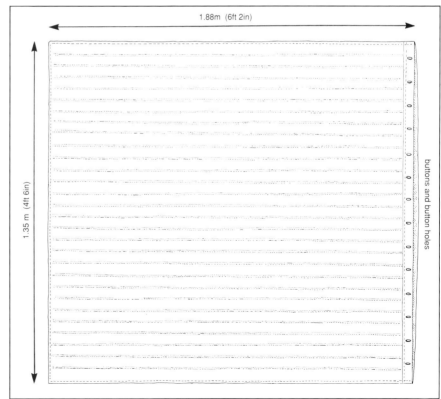

1.88m (6ft 2in)

1.35 m (4ft 6in)

buttons and button holes

25

cushion front with a 1cm (1½in) seam allowance. At one short end (42cm/17in) pin frill 2cm (¾in) away from raw edge and not on edge (this is because we have to stitch the Velcro here). Make sure piped side of frill is face down. Machine stitch frill in place using zipper foot.

4 At the short end, where the frill is 2cm (¾in) away from raw edge, pin a 25cm (10in) strip of Velcro so it is in the middle of the side. The Velcro edge must be level with raw edge of cushion cover. Machine stitch around four sides of this Velcro.

5 Take the back side of the cushion cover and machine stitch Velcro onto its right side in the same way as you have just done to the front of the cushion cover.

6 Pin back side to front side, raw edges and right sides together. At the Velcro ends you need to fold the Velcro back on itself, wrong sides together. Pin. Machine around the three other sides of cover with zipper foot and along the fourth side, machine up to the Velcro at both its ends. It is vital that this line of stitching is inside any previous lines of stitching. Hence no previous ones will show when you turn this cover, right sides out.

7 Trim seams and oversew. Turn cover. Press.

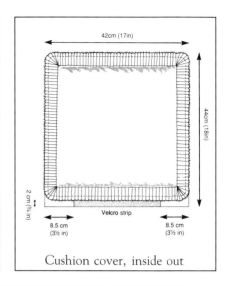

Cushion cover, inside out

LEFT *Ingenious use of antique linen and lace has created pretty coverings for both bed and window.*

ABOVE *Blue piping around the frilled cushion covers gives subtle definition to an otherwise simple bedroom.*

4

BED VALANCES

The bed valance (U.S., 'dust ruffle') deserves all the special attention and
decisions that you would apply to any other detail in your bedroom. Just because
it is around the bottom of the bed, and possibly partially covered by your
bedcover, does not mean that it should be anything less than beautiful and made
out of the best material possible (in terms of colour and texture).

CHOOSING A BED VALANCE

You may well have a situation in your
bedroom where the curtains, pelmets,
corona and even a small chair or dressing table are all done in a heavenly
printed chintz or another patterned
fabric. If so, it is vital to counter-
balance all the patterns with a material that is a solid colour, or else two
or three plain colours. You may then
well feel that doing the headboard,
and possibly the inside lining of a
corona in this contrasting material
would be an excellent decision. It
would all lend itself perfectly to the
overall harmony and balance in the
room.

There are many possible designs for
a valance, ranging from plain geometric shapes to gathered looks which
give a softer effect. Eight of these are
explained in the following pages,
namely:

- Kick-pleated: the simplest and most
  economical to produce
- Gathered skirt: pretty and soft
- Close box-pleated: smart and tailored, but uses a lot of material
- Spaced box-pleated: wider spaces between the pleats
- Box-pleated, off a piped band: best
  for bed bases which are high off the
  floor
- Gathered, off a piped band: softer
  look for higher beds
- Gathered, with a ruched, piped
  band
- Box-pleated, with triangular points:
  clever, geometric and modern.

General points

1 Always line a valance. They look so
much better, and it also makes the
making-up process easy, especially
when you get to the hem.

2 Never interline them – it is point-
less. You would never use interlining
when dealing with kick or box pleats.
They need to look sharp and tailored
and interlining would spoil this.
Equally, interlining would ruin the
look of a gathered valance which
should look light and pretty. Interlining is important for curtains: to enhance the thick, lavish look of the
window treatment; to block sunlight
coming from behind which fades curtains; and to increase the insulation in
the room. None of these applies to a
valance.

3 Always make a lip (to go around the
edge of the horizontal part of the bed
base) of at least 12cm (5in) finished
size. This is so you never see the unattractive lining (which goes over the
horizontal part of the bed base) at the
very edge of the mattress: you see the
lovely chintz, or whatever, instead.

4 Always pipe the seam where the
skirt joins the lip. This gives the item
a professional finishing touch.

5 Always make a flap, attached to the
head end of the valance, to slip down
the back of the bed base. This helps
keep the valance in place.

6 The hem on your valance must
never be less than 4cm (1½in). This
makes it hang well (similar to a hem
on a dress or coat).

If you use the following instructions
there will be not one seam exposed
when the valance is finished. It will
look as neat and beautiful at the back
as it does from the front.

MEASURING UP

Get your long 2m (6ft) folding
wooden ruler, and push it between the
bed base and the mattress, about 4cm
(1½in) in from the edge, along the
long side of the bed. Make sure you
take the ruler right to the foot and
head edge of the bed, over the top of
the piping (which is the place where
the horizontal base meets the vertical
sides). Next, measure the short side,
across the bed, at the foot end, again
about 4cm (1½in) in from the edge.

Ignore the fact that the bed base has
a curved corner as opposed to a sharp,
pointed, right angle at the corner.
When you are making your valance
you will see that it will also have a
natural curve at its corners which will
conveniently fit the lines of the bed
base.

Now measure the exact drop of the
bed, from the top of the base to the
carpet or wooden boards.

The quantity of material needed
now entirely depends on what style of
valance you choose. Tables 1 and 2
(pages 30 and 31) will guide you.

*A valance can add the perfect finishing
touch to bedroom furnishings. Box
pleats are an authentic choice here, to
tie in beautifully with the needlepoint
cushions and pictures.*

TABLE 1
Bed Valance Material Quantities

Style		Single 75cm 2ft 6in	Single 90cm 3ft	Double 1.35m 4ft 6in	Double 1.50m 5ft	Double 1.65m 5ft 6in	Double 1.80m 6ft
Kick-pleated	m	3.7	4.0	4.5	5.0	5.3	5.8
	yd	4.1	4.4	5.0	5.5	5.8	6.4
No. widths for skirt		4	4	5	5	5	5
Gathered skirt	m	5.3	5.7	6.3	6.9	7.5	8.0
	yd	5.8	6.3	6.9	7.6	8.2	8.8
No. widths for skirt		8	8	9	9	9	10
Close box-pleated	m	6.1	6.5	7.5	7.8	8.3	8.7
	yd	6.7	7.1	8.2	8.5	9.1	9.5
No. widths for skirt		10	10	11	11	12	12
Spaced box-pleated	m	6.1	6.5	7.5	7.8	8.3	8.7
	yd	6.7	7.1	8.2	8.5	9.1	9.5
No. widths for skirt		10	10	11	11	12	12
Box-pleated; off piped band	m	6.7	7.1	8.1	8.4	8.9	9.3
	yd	7.4	7.8	8.9	9.2	9.8	10.2
No. widths for skirt		10	10	11	11	12	12
Gathered; off piped band	m	6.1	6.5	7.5	7.8	8.3	8.7
	yd	6.7	7.1	8.2	8.5	9.1	9.5
No. widths for skirt		8	8	9	9	9	10
Gathered; ruched piped band	m	6.9	7.3	8.3	8.6	9.1	9.5
	yd	7.6	8.0	9.1	9.4	10.0	10.4
No. widths for skirt		8	8	9	9	9	10
Box-pleated; triangular points	m	7.8	8.2	8.8	9.4	10.0	10.5
	yd	8.5	9.0	9.6	10.3	11.0	11.5
No. widths for skirt		8	8	9	9	9	10

This table assumes you are using plain or fairly uncomplicated material, so you do not have to allow too much extra for pattern repeats.

You are allowing for five sets of kick pleats: one in the centre of the two longer sides, one at each foot-end corner, and one in the centre of the foot end.

Lip: 2 strips 1.93m × 15cm (6ft 5in × 5in); 1 strip 1.4m × 15cm (4ft 8in × 5in)

Flap at head end: 1.38m × 43cm (4ft 7in × 17in)

Piping (cut on the bias): 1 strip 5.26m × 4cm (5¾yd × 1½in)

Lining for skirt: 6.3m × 33cm (7yd × 13in)

Lining for horizontal base: 1.92m × 1.38m (6ft 5in × 4ft 7in)

1 Make up piping so it is ready for when you need to include it. Join strips together to make one long strip to cover the cord. Press the seams of the strips open (see page 21).

2 Fold in 1.5cm (½in) at the beginning and end of the strip and place the cord in the centre of the wrong side of the strip, with the ends tucked under the turn-backs. Fold the strip over the cord, matching the raw edges. Machine stitch close to the cord. Always use a zipper foot on your sewing machine so you can stitch really close to the cord.

3 Lay the valance base (cut from lining) on your work table (or else a large floor space) and 'set up' the lip.

KICK-PLEATED VALANCE

This valance is the plainest, the simplest to make, and the most economical to produce. It is totally straight, with no gathers. Its interest is only in the kick pleats at its corners and half-way down its two long sides. If you are making a kick-pleated valance for a double bed you should also put a pleat half-way across the foot of the bed – an essential detail to break up the long stretch of material.

The sample valance
Bed size, standard double: 1.88m × 1.35m (6ft 2in × 4ft 6in); drop 34cm (13½in)

Cut material for

Skirt: 6.3m × 41cm (7yd × 16½in)

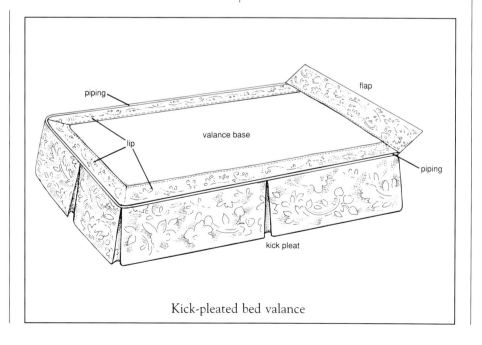

Kick-pleated bed valance

TABLE 2
Bed Valance Lining Quantities

Style		Single 75cm 2ft 6in	Single 90cm 3ft	Double 1.35m 4ft 6in	Double 1.50m 5ft	Double 1.65m 5ft 6in	Double 1.80m 6ft
Kick-pleated	m	4.1	4.4	4.9	7.4	7.7	8.0
	yd	4.5	4.8	5.4	8.0	8.5	8.8
Gathered skirt	m	5.7	6.1	6.7	9.3	9.9	10.4
	yd	6.2	6.7	7.3	10.2	10.8	11.4
Close box-pleated	m	6.0	6.5	7.4	9.7	10.2	10.7
	yd	6.6	7.1	8.1	10.6	11.2	11.7
Spaced box-pleated	m	6.0	6.5	7.4	9.7	10.2	10.7
	yd	6.6	7.1	8.1	10.6	11.2	11.7
Box-pleated; off piped band	m	6.6	7.0	8.0	8.3	8.8	9.2
	yd	7.2	7.7	8.8	9.1	9.6	10.1
Gathered; off piped band	m	6.0	6.4	7.4	7.7	8.2	8.6
	yd	6.6	7.0	8.1	8.4	9.0	9.4
Gathered; ruched piped band	m	6.0	6.4	7.4	7.7	8.2	8.6
	yd	6.6	7.0	8.1	8.4	9.0	9.4
Box-pleated; triangular points	m	5.7	6.1	6.7	9.3	9.9	10.4
	yd	6.2	6.7	7.3	10.2	10.8	11.4

side edge of the lip. You then machine stitch the piping on to the lip, with a 1.5cm (½in) seam, using your zipper foot. Do not trim or notch the seam at this stage. Put the piped lip to one side while you make up the skirt for the valance.

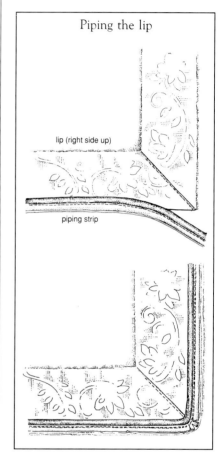

Piping the lip

This means you want to lay the strips cut especially for the lip on the lining base. Put one of the long strips along the base's longest side, wrong side down, with the raw edges together. Make sure the strip is exactly the same length as the lining for the base. Now do the same down the other long side, and across the narrow side at the foot end. There is no need to pin at this stage. If you are working on a table, clamps will help you enormously, holding the lip, temporarily, in place on the base.

4 Turn under the ends of the shortest strip at the foot end, to form a perfectly angled mitre across the longer strip.

5 Pin the angled fold of the lip material (not the base – you have just been using it as a guide) and then press the fold, using a closed pair of scissors: run the closed blade of your scissors along the pinned seam. This is a quick and effective way of making a crease without using a hot iron. Repeat process at the other corner.

6 Now top stitch the seam at each corner (sewing the lip only), using matching thread colour. It is vital to

stop stitches 2cm (¾in) from the inside corner as you have to turn the edge of the lip under later. Press. Trim away seam at back to 1cm (½in).

7 With right sides together, pin the ready-made piping to the lip by matching the raw edges of the covered piping along the raw edge of the out-

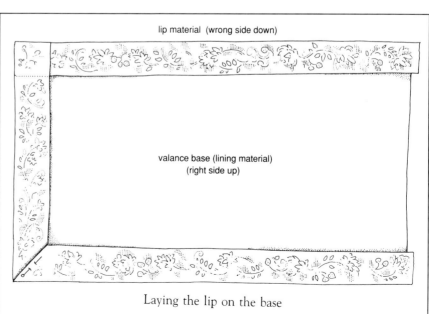

Laying the lip on the base

8 Join together all the vertical seams of the skirt by stitching them, right sides together, with a 1.5cm (½in) seam allowance. Press the seam open with a hot iron. Repeat this whole process with the lining material.

9 Along the long hem edge of the valance skirt, place together the raw edges of the material and the lining, right sides together. Machine stitch seam with a 1.5cm (½in) seam allowance. Stop stitching 7cm (2¾in) before either end, so that you will be able to hand stitch up the sides, once you have turned the skirt.

10 Once they are attached to each other, turn the material and the lining so that their right sides are out and their raw edges are level at the top. Do not worry if your raw edges are not level. Having checked that the drop of the skirt is now exactly the finished drop from the top of the bed base to the floor, plus 1.5cm (½in) seam allowance, merely trim off any excess lining at the top. Press the hem end with great care. (The hem turn-up on the wrong side should be 4cm (1½in) all the way along.)

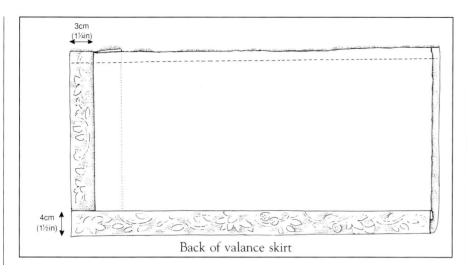

3cm
(1¼in)

4cm
(1½in)

Back of valance skirt

11 Turn in approximately 5cm (2in) of the outer material up the sides of the two ends of the skirt. Pin. Then turn under the lining to leave approximately a 3cm (1¼in) gap between the folded edges of the two. Slip stitch the lining to the outer material.

12 Machine stitch along the raw edges at the top of the skirt to marry the lining and the material together.

13 Take the piped lip and mark out, with pins, where each kick pleat is to go – exactly in the centre of each long side, and in the centre of the foot end. Each kick pleat should be 5cm (2in) deep on each side of the central mark. Now mark out one kick pleat at each corner of the bottom end of the valance. Half a pleat – 5cm (2in) – will be on the long side of the bed, and the other half will be on the short side, with the corner in between.

Having marked out the beginnings, ends and middles of the five pleats, now cut notches in the seam allowance of the lip exactly where each pin is. Then remove the pins. This will now enable you to make your kick pleats without any trouble at all, when you attach the valance skirt to the lip.

LEFT, ABOVE *Gathered skirt valances in a floral fabric are offset by the plain white bed linen.*

LEFT *A simple kick-pleated valance is the obvious choice for this modest room.*

Making a kick pleat

piped lip

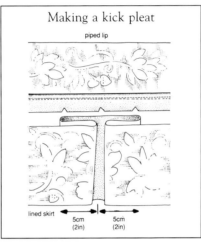

lined skirt

5cm
(2in)

5cm
(2in)

14 Place the right sides of the skirt and the lip together. Stitch together using zipper foot. When you get to a notch, make a kick pleat, by folding 5cm (2in) of the skirt back on itself once and then again in reverse, using the notches to guide the beginning and end of each pleat.

When you get to making the kick pleats at the corners, leave a 1cm (⅜in) gap at the centre between the two halves of the kick pleat (that is, at the very corner of the lip). This will enable each kick pleat to hang absolutely 'plumb' before the corner is actually turned. Pin the lower edges of the kick pleats in place, and press hard.

15 Now put the wrong side of the bed base to the wrong side of the skirt, now stitched to the piped lip.

It is wise to start pinning this from the foot end, and work upwards towards the head end. This is because if you have an excess of skirt, or bed base lining, it is easier to adjust it at the head end than at the foot end of the bed.

16 With the skirt pinned to the base, machine stitch with zipper foot, with a seam allowance of 1.5cm (½in). Press and trim seams down to 1cm (⅜in). Notch corners.

17 Turn the lip back right side out, so it folds neatly over all the raw edges. Fold under the inside edge of the lip, so that the size of the finished lip is approximately 12cm (5in). Top stitch in matching colour.

18 For the back flap, pin the material strip with its right side to the wrong side of the base at the head end, then stitch. On other long side of flap, press 1.5cm (½in) over from right side to wrong. Then fold the flap in half longways, so that its right sides are touching, lining up the edge of the fold with the seam you have just stitched. Machine stitch with a 1.5cm (½in)

Stitching lip and skirt to base

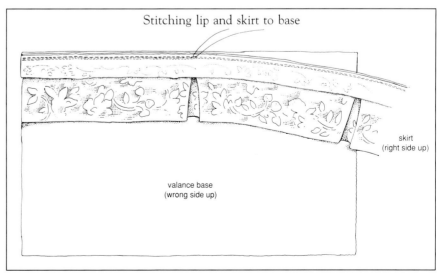

skirt
(right side up)

valance base
(wrong side up)

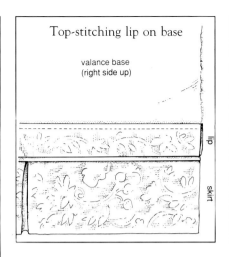

Top-stitching lip on base

valance base
(right side up)

lip

skirt

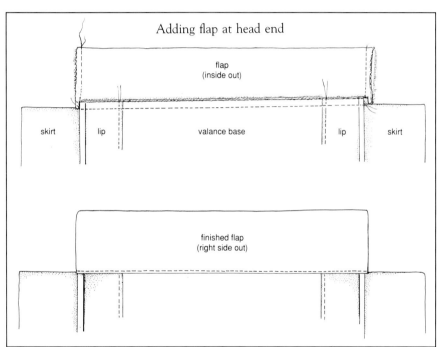

Adding flap at head end

flap
(inside out)

skirt

lip

valance base

lip

skirt

finished flap
(right side out)

throughout the room. For example, if you already have a very gathered pelmet on your window and on your corona, and even on the dressing table or bedroom chairs, don't then swamp the room with more frills in the bed valance. At that point you would choose a simpler, more tailored look.

However, let's assume you have got the balance right and a gathered-skirt valance is perfect. It is slightly more extravagant than the kick-pleated one, since you have to allow material for 2½ times around the three sides of the bed base. But, in a sense, it is easier to execute since gathering up

the skirt (once you have got the hang of it) is a lot more straightforward than measuring out kick pleats and going around corners with them.

The sample valance

Bed size, standard double: 1.88m × 1.35m (6ft 2in × 4ft 6in); drop 34cm (13½in)

Cut material for

Skirt: 12.8m × 41cm (14yd × 16½in)

Lip: 2 strips 1.93 × 15cm (6ft 5in × 5in); 1 strip 1.4m × 15cm (4ft 8in × 5in)

Flap at head end: 1.38m × 43cm (4ft 7in × 17in)

Piping (cut on the bias): 1 strip 5.26m × 4cm (5¾yd × 1½in)

Lining for skirt: 12.8m × 33cm (14 yd × 13in)

Lining for horizontal base: 1.92m × 1.38m (6ft 5in × 4ft 7in)

1–12 Follow steps as for a kick-pleated valance (pages 30–3).

13 Gather up the skirt, going over the row of machine stitches at the raw edge of the lining and the outer material. Gathering is done by hand as the skirt is fed through the machine. The technique used in dressmaking of pulling up long, loose machine stitches is not possible when making such a long length of gathers. Making the gathers even would be very time consuming, and the threads would inevitably break at some point while being pulled

seam allowance down each short side.

You have now made a wide, shallow pocket. Turn this inside out, so that the open edge of the flap is now on the upper (lip) side of valance. Press. Pin long already folded edge and machine stitch in place with correct colour. Press.

GATHERED-SKIRT VALANCE

This has a completely different character to the kick-pleated valance. It is pretty and feminine to look at, with a soft and subtle character. If that is the look you want, this is the correct design to choose. But be careful not to overdo the gathered, frilled look

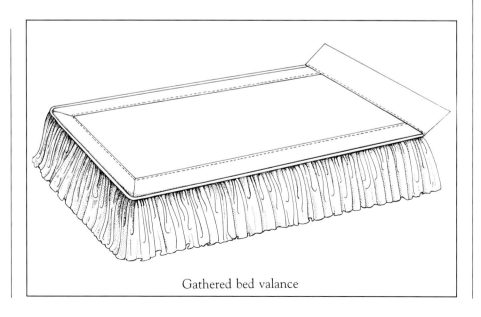

Gathered bed valance

A lovely, tightly gathered valance, behaving perfectly despite its long drop. The skirt starts and stops at the foot-end posts, and is piped, which adds a professional touch.

over the long lengths needed for the frill.

Gathering while machine stitching is an easy technique to pick up, and needs only a little practice on scraps of material. If you feel unsure about how much to gather in order to get the correct length of gathered skirt, insert a pin every 25cm (10in) in the raw edge of the skirt. Each 25cm (10in) section must then be gathered up into 10cm (4in) of finished skirt. Check as you go along, and make adjustments as necessary.

14 Once the skirt is gathered correctly, place the right sides of the skirt and the lip together. Stitch together using the zipper foot.

15–18 Follow steps as for kick-pleated valance (pages 33–4).

CLOSE BOX-PLEATED VALANCE

This valance is fairly extravagant on material as you must allow 3 times around the three sides of the bed base. It is an extremely smart, tailored valance but it also has a delightfully old-fashioned look. Like a kick-pleated valance it is perfect when everything else in the room is fairly gathered and frilled.

Work out how wide you would like each box pleat to be. It is a question of personal taste, but I would highly recommend that each pleat should be approximately 9cm (3½in) wide. However, if an 8cm (3in) or a 10cm (4in) box pleat suits the width of your bed better, they will still look perfect. I would be tempted to go neither narrower than 8cm (3in) nor wider than 10cm (4in)

The sample valance
Bed size, standard double: 1.88m × 1.35m (6ft 2in × 4ft 6in); drop 34cm (13½in)

Cut material for

Skirt: 15.5m × 41cm (17yd × 16½in)

Lip: 2 strips 1.93m × 15cm (6ft 5in × 5in); 1 strip 1.4m × 15cm (4ft 8in × 5in)

Flap at head end: 1.38m × 43cm (4ft 7in × 17in)

Piping (cut on the bias): 1 strip 5.26m × 4cm (5¾yd × 1½in)

Lining for skirt: 15.5m × 33cm (17yd × 13in)

Lining for horizontal base: 1.92m × 1.38m (6ft 5in × 4ft 7in)

1–12 Follow steps as for a kick-pleated valance (pages 30–3).

13 Take your already piped lip. You are going to mark out, with notches, the outside edge of the lip: these notches will then guide you as to where you start and finish each box pleat. Measure the lip at the foot end, between the machine stitching of the piping. For our standard bed (as given above) it will measure 1.35m. Now divide this number by 12 which equals 11.25cm. This means there will be 12 pleats, measuring 11.25cm wide.

Now mark out on the foot end of the lip, with pins, exactly where each pleat is going to start and finish. Check, and then cut a notch on the lip at each pin. It is then essential to

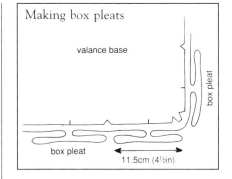

Making box pleats

valance base

box pleat

box pleat

11.5cm (4½in)

mark out the middle of each pleat as well. It is advisable to do this particular 'central' mark with a pen, so that it differs from the notches, which indicate the beginning and end of each pleat. Make absolutely sure you have a notch, i.e. the right side of the fold of the box pleat, ½cm (⅛in) before each of the bottom corners of the bed. Make your next notch ½cm (⅛in) from the corner, on the long side of the bed. Repeat this notching and pen-marking process up the two long sides so that they will also be prepared for their box pleats.

14 Take the very long, lined, but still unpleated skirt, and lay it right sides together with the lip, matching their raw edges together. Make box pleat between the first two notches, using your essential pen mark as a guide for the centre of the pleat. Pin as you go.

At the corner it is *vital* that on the wrong side there is now a box pleat facing you (which means there is obviously an inverted pleat, like a kick pleat, on the right side). It is essential to start pleating the correct way so that when you reach the first notch at the corner you have come to the end of a box pleat. You can now turn the corner with ease with your next box pleat.

Machine stitch skirt to lip using the zipper foot.

15–18 Follow steps as for kick-pleated valance (pages 33–4).

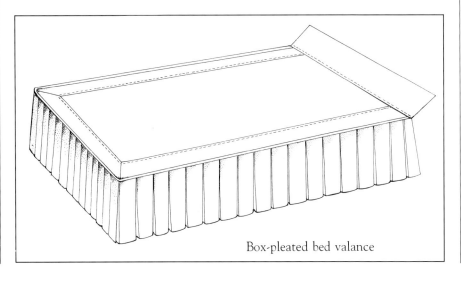

Box-pleated bed valance

A contrast-bound, spaced box-pleated valance, which ties in beautifully with the headboard, cushions and curtains.

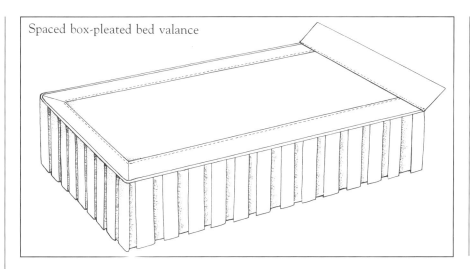

Spaced box-pleated bed valance

SPACED BOX-PLEATED VALANCE

This is very similar to the close box-pleated valance. Its only difference is that there is a space in between each pleat. This obviously gives a less full look and uses up slightly less material for the skirt.

The sample valance

Bed size, standard double: 1.88m × 1.35m (6ft 2in × 4ft 6in); drop 34cm (13½in)

Cut material for

Skirt: 15.5m × 41cm (17yd × 16½in)

Lip: 2 strips 1.93m × 15cm (6ft 5in × 5in); 1 strip 1.4m × 15cm (4ft 8in × 5in)

Flap at head end: 1.38m × 43cm (4ft 7in × 17in)

Piping (cut on the bias): 1 strip 5.26m × 4cm (5¾yd × 1½in)

Lining for skirt: 15.5m × 33cm (17yd × 13in)

Lining for horizontal base: 1.92m × 1.38m (6ft 5in × 4ft 7in)

1–12 Follow steps as for a kick-pleated valance (pages 30–3). However, you will have to finish the ends of the skirt (at the head end of the bed) (step 11) after you have worked out your pleats and gaps, and know how much material is going to be taken up by the skirt.

13 Follow step 13 as for close box-pleated valance, above. The only difference is that you mark out specific gaps between each box pleat. For example, if your box pleats are 9cm (3½in) wide, leave a gap of 5cm (2in) between each pleat.

Bearing this in mind, follow the instructions for the close box-pleated valance.

14 Follow step 14 as for close box-pleated valance, leaving gaps between pleats, and taking care to turn corner correctly with a pleat.

15–18 Follow steps as for kick-pleated valance (pages 33–4).

BOX-PLEATED VALANCE OFF A PIPED BAND

This is the perfect valance for a bed base that is fairly high off the floor, i.e. approximately 40–45cm (16–18in) from top of base to floor.

The reason for this is that if you want a box-pleated valance on a bed this high, your valance skirt needs to be more than just box pleats. You cannot expect very long box pleats to hang sharply and correctly for the rest of their life. Valances have a certain amount of stress which a pelmet never has: feet cannot help kicking valances while the bed is being made, so pleats will inevitably get disturbed. The answer for this is to reduce the length of the box pleats to an approximate length of 30–35cm (12–14in) and hang them off a piped band. The box

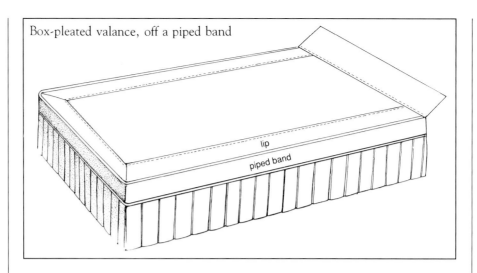

Box-pleated valance, off a piped band

lip

piped band

pleats will now hang correctly, and retain their shape for longer.

The sample valance
Finished size of band: 8cm (3¼in); skirt 26cm (10¼in)

Bed size, standard double: 1.88m × 1.35m (6ft 2in × 4ft 6in); drop 34cm (13½in)

Cut material for

Skirt: 15.5m × 33cm (17yd × 13in)

Band: 5.2m × 11cm (5yd 2ft × 4½in)

Lip: 2 strips 1.93m × 15cm (6ft 5in × 5in); 1 strip 1.4m × 15cm (4ft 8in × 5in)

Flap at head end: 1.38m × 43cm (4ft 7in × 17in)

Piping (cut on the bias): 2 strips 5.26m × 4cm (5¾yd × 1½in) each

Lining for skirt: 15.5m × 25cm (17yd × 10in)

Lining for band: 5.2m × 11cm (5yd 2ft × 4½in)

Lining for horizontal base: 1.92m × 1.38m (6ft 5in × 4ft 7in)

1–12 Follow steps as for a kick-pleated valance (pages 30–3).

13 Now prepare the band. (Its lining will be added later.) Join the seams. Press open and trim. Pipe its lower edge, as you have already done on the lip, matching raw edges together in the usual way.

14 Join band to piped lip, placing right sides of band and lip together. Machine stitch with zipper foot.

15 Notch and mark with a pen the lower edge of the band, so that it is ready for its box-pleated skirt.

Now follow steps 14 and 15 as for a box-pleated valance (page 36), except that you are joining the skirt to the band, not the lip.

16 Join the seams of lining for the band. Match the right side of its long raw edge with the skirt and band raw edge (which are now machined together). Stitch band lining along the same machine line of the box-pleated skirt. Trim seam and press lining up so that its other raw edge is level with the top of the material-band raw edge, which is stitched to the lip. Machine stitch together with zipper foot. Trim and press.

Now follow steps 16–18, as for kick-pleated valance (pages 33–4).

GATHERED VALANCE OFF PIPED BAND

An extremely pretty valance and another design suitable for beds which are fairly high off the ground: 40–45cm (16–18in). This one has all the same characteristics as those discussed in the gathered-skirt valance (page 00), but it has a slightly more organised look to it than the ordinary gathered skirt.

The sample valance
Finished size of band: 8cm (3¼in); skirt 26cm (10¼in)

Bed size, standard double: 1.88m × 1.35m (6ft 2in × 4ft 6in); drop 34cm (13½in)

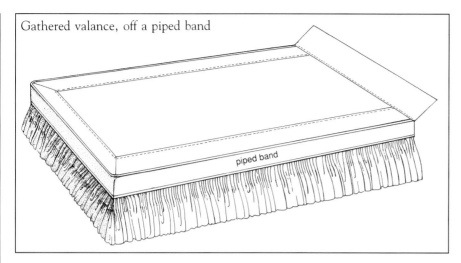

Gathered valance, off a piped band

piped band

Cut material for

Skirt: 12.8m × 33cm (14yd × 13in)

Band: 5.2m × 11cm (5yd 2ft × 4½in)

Lip: 2 strips 1.93m × 15cm (6ft 5in × 5in); 1 strip 1.4m × 15cm (4ft 8in × 5in)

Flap at head end: 1.38m × 43cm (4ft 7in × 17in)

Piping (cut on the bias): 2 strips 5.26m × 4cm (5¾yd × 1½in) each

Lining for skirt: 12.8m × 25cm (14 yd × 10in)

Lining for band: 5.2m × 11cm (5yd 2ft × 4½in)

Lining for horizontal base: 1.92m × 1.38m (6ft 5in × 4ft 7in)

1–12 Follow steps as for a kick-pleated valance (pages 30–3).

13–14 Follow steps as for box-pleated valance off a piped band (page 38).

15 Now prepare the skirt in exactly the same way as you would for step 13 of a gathered-skirt valance (page 34).

16 Once the skirt is gathered correctly, join it to the bottom edge of the band, right sides together.

17 Join the seams of lining for the band. Match the right side of its long raw edge with the skirt and band raw edge (which are now machined together). Stitch band lining along the same machine line of the box-pleated skirt. Trim seam and press lining up so that its other raw edge is level with the top of the material-band raw edge, which is stitched to the lip. Machine stitch together with zipper foot. Trim and press.

Now follow steps 16–18, as for kick-pleated valance (pages 33–4).

GATHERED VALANCE WITH A RUCHED PIPED BAND

This is extremely similar to the previous valance with all the same characteristics. The ruched band is merely an added detail which adds an even greater dimension to the overall look of the valance.

The sample valance
Finished size of band: 8cm (3¼in); skirt 26cm (10¼in)
Bed size, standard double: 1.88m × 1.35m (6ft 2in × 4ft 6in); drop 34cm (13½in)

Cut material for

Skirt: 12.8m × 33cm (14yd × 13in)

Band: 15.6m × 11cm (17yd × 4½in)

Lip: 2 strips 1.93m × 15cm (6ft 5in × 5in); 1 strip 1.4m × 15cm (4ft 8in × 5in)

Flap at head end: 1.38m × 43cm (4ft 7in × 17in)

Piping (cut on the bias): 2 strips 5.26m × 4cm (5¾yd × 1½in) each

Lining for skirt: 12.8m × 25cm (14yd × 10in)

Lining for band: 5.2m × 11cm (5yd 2ft × 4½in)

Lining for horizontal base: 1.92m × 1.38m (6ft 5in × 4ft 7in)

Follow the instructions for the gathered valance off a piped band (pages 38–9).

The only difference is in the band itself which is gathered on each edge before being attached to the lip and the skirt. The material for this must be cut three times the length of the three sides of the bed, and it also needs to be a bit wider: instead of allowing for two seams of 1.5cm (½in), make one (the left-hand side as you take it through the sewing machine) 3cm (1¼in).

The extra width will help enormously when you are gathering up the second edge of the ruched band – it will help your fingertips guide the band through the machine. You can then trim the left-hand side off to a normal seam allowance of 1.5cm (½in). The gathering is done by hand on the machine in exactly the same way as the skirt is gathered in. (See page 21.) Make sure that you run the band through the machine in the same direction for both sides. Do not stitch down one side, go across the bottom and then up the other side, or the

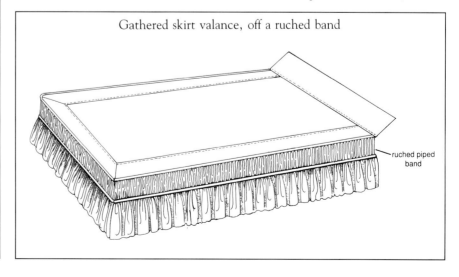

Gathered skirt valance, off a ruched band

ruched piped band

resulting gathers could look very skewed and unattractive.

BOX-PLEATED VALANCE WITH TRIANGULAR POINTS

This valance has a wonderfully geometric character: highly organised, very modern and most attractive. It looks incredibly complicated and clever when it is, in fact, extremely straightforward.

It looks best if the box pleats with their points have gaps between them, as opposed to being closely placed. Close box pleats would look overpowering. To look at from the outside the box pleats should be 5cm (2in) wide (i.e. 10cm (4in) total length). There should be a 4cm (1½in) gap between each pleat.

Because of the construction of the points you use a double layer of material for the skirt of this valance, rather than material and lining.

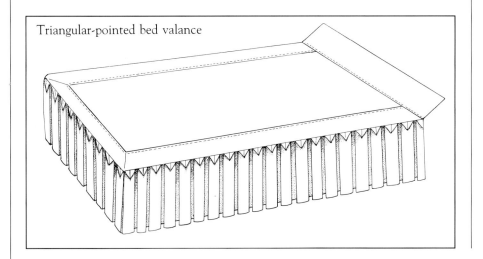

Triangular-pointed bed valance

The sample valance

Bed size, standard double: 1.88m × 1.35m (6ft 2in × 4ft 6in); drop 34cm (13½in)

Cut material for

Skirt: 12.8m × 75cm (14yd × 29½in)

Lip: 2 strips 1.93m × 15cm (6ft 5in × 5in); 1 strip 1.4m × 15cm (4ft 8in × 5in)

Flap at head end: 1.38m × 43cm (4ft 7in × 17in)

Piping (cut on the bias): 1 strip 5.26m × 4cm (5¾yd × 1½in)

Lining for horizontal base: 1.92m × 1.38m (6ft 5in × 4ft 7in)

1–7 Follow steps for a kick-pleated valance (pages 30–1).

8 Fold the skirt material, longways, right sides together, with raw edges level. Machine along raw edges with a seam allowance of 1.5cm (½in). Turn a right angle when you get to the end and machine up the short side. (You will in fact eventually cut off this seam. You want to do this purely to ease the situation when you turn your skirt right sides out.)

9 Turn skirt right sides out by pushing against the closed end with something long and thin like a broom handle. When it is totally turned, cut off the seam up the short side.

10 Press the skirt in such a way that you have a 4cm (1½in) turn-up along the bottom edge. Now you have no seam at the top edge, which is excellent because you do not want any bulky seam in your way when you are

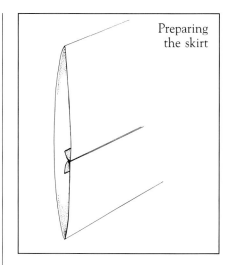

Preparing the skirt

making the points at the top of the box pleats. Turn in the two end seams, on each other. Slip stitch the first end invisibly, but don't do the other end yet: you may want to cut off a bit of skirt when you come to that end.

11 Notch up the lip in the same way as in step 13 of the spaced box-pleated valance (page 38), but remember you need to leave a gap between each pleat.

12 Take the skirt, now ready for box pleating, and carefully pin it to the lip, right sides together, arranging the box pleats as you go.

13 Having pinned each pleat, very carefully remove the pleated skirt from the lip, but keep the pins in place which are holding down the box pleats. Press the pinned pleats to achieve a sharp line. Remove pins and instead place a pin horizontally across a sharp line at the base of the pleat. Stitch halfway down each pleat.

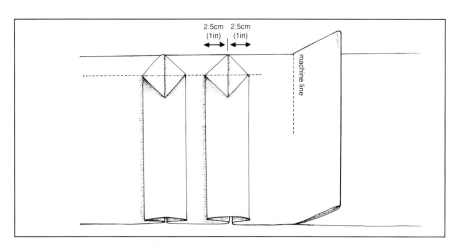

14 Working from top to bottom, pin each pleat flat on the right side of the valance skirt, placing the seam exactly in the middle. It's absolutely vital that your pleats are exactly even, so use your small ruler to check that the seam is in the middle of each pleat (i.e. 2.5cm (1in) from each side). Put two pins at the top and two at the bottom of each pleat. Press the pleats, leaving the pins in. (Do not use plastic-headed pins, or the heat will melt them on to the material.)

Then, staying at the ironing board, remove the pins from the first pleat, and pull the front of the pleat down to form a diamond shape, and press. Stitch each diamond down at its low-est point with a hand stitch in the correct colour thread.

Repeat for each pleat.

15 When all the diamonds have been hand stitched down, machine stitch in a continuous horizontal line, parallel to the top, through the middle of each diamond. This line is going to be your exact seam line when you join the skirt to the lip. It is important that the diamond shape is held securely in place. Trim the upper edge of the skirt, cutting off the tops of the diamonds, to 1.5cm (½in).

16 Feed the skirt on to the lip, right sides together. Your beautiful box pleats should correspond exactly to

This gathered valance complements the plainer bedcover, and cleverly echoes the skirt around the chair near the window. Note the use of flower rosettes (see page 103) on the curtains and the corona.

your notched and marked lip. Now machine stitch *exactly* on top of line in step 15, but *never* waver above it, since the stitches would then be exposed on the front of the pleated skirt, when you turn it.

Now follow steps 15–18 as for kick-pleated valance (pages 33–4).

5

BEDCOVERS

Covering your bed with a co-ordinated cover is a finishing touch that sets the tone of a room in a substantial way. The bed, and the room, look tidy and neat as soon as the bedcover is thrown over, and I would consider one to be essential, unless your duvet cover is very beautiful. The bedcover is also an essential element of your overall bedroom design, and can balance other items such as a gathered bed valance, a buttoned headboard or an elaborate corona.

PLAIN WHITE BEDCOVERS

If you already have a lot of printed material or patterned chintz in your bedroom – in the curtains and pelmets, valance or headboard – then you will want to contrast and balance all this with some solid and unfussy design. Heavy, white, woven cotton bedcovers look brilliant in this situation, and you can buy one from any large department store. White cotton bedcovers are very easy to look after: they do not crease and they love the washing machine.

Even better than this, though, try and find an old one from an antique shop or market stall specialising in old linen. If you happen to find one that is just too narrow for your bed but, apart from that, perfect, don't despair. Find some wonderful heavy cotton lace or light linen fringe and machine it on all the way round. I did exactly this: I bought a *beautiful* bedcover in the Provence market of Isle-sur-la-Sorgue which was a tiny bit too narrow. I could have bought some lace or fringing but, even better, I was able to order some heavy cotton lace, about 10cm (5in) wide, with a scalloped edge (made in the Eastern Highlands of Zimbabwe where I happened to be on holiday – see list of suppliers). It is perfect and absolutely 'makes' the bedcover.

CHINTZ BEDCOVERS

A chintz bedcover is usually equally stunning in an elegant bedroom. It looks beautiful when the bedcover matches chintz curtains and perhaps the headboard; and there is a contrasting bed valance, and bedside tables or dressing tables which are covered in something that is different to chintz.

Quilted bedcovers

Quilted chintz bedcovers look particularly good because any form of quilting process on chintz introduces depth to the print. Also, on a practical note, they are easy to handle (the Dacron used for quilting is much lighter than medium-weight interlining), and even though they are folded every night they never crease.

Never attempt to quilt a bedcover yourself. It is honestly not possible – even if you think it is! I did it once – and once only. It is such a mistake, and the trouble is once you start it you have to finish it. There is no going back and it is virtually impossible to manoeuvre the sheer size of the item around your domestic sewing machine. It is far better to send it to a commercial quilter who will do it for you (see list of suppliers on page 124).

It is easiest to send your length of chintz direct from the material retailer. You then order whichever pattern of quilting you want: outline, onion, diamond, squared, or parallel lines. They quilt the material for you and send it back on its bolt, ready for you to make your bedcover. Do not worry about the fact that there is now a bulky edge to the material (exactly where you want to pattern-match). With very sharp scissors, trim away all the Dacron possible at edges so you can now pattern-match with ease.

One company will quilt up in any of these designs but they also pattern-match and join up your bedcover seams for you (see suppliers list). Thus, when it is sent back, all you have to do is curve its two foot-end corners (to be explained later) and line it (see steps 17–20, page 46).

Plain chintz bedcovers

A simple chintz bedcover – absolutely plain – also looks wonderful. Naturally, it is the cheapest and, in a sense, the easiest to achieve in comparison to the types already mentioned, as it does not involve any expensive purchases, not do you pay for any quilting process.

You must use medium bump to interline a plain bedcover. Do not use domette: it is too thin and the cover will crease up easily. Nor should you use heavy bump as you will find it a nightmare to handle since it is so heavy. The medium is perfect: thick enough to stop the chintz creasing, yet light enough to handle.

MAKING A BEDCOVER

It is essential that you allow at least a metre (3ft 3in) extra length, so that you have a generous quantity to go over the pillows. It also looks good if

An attractive, diamond-quilted bedcover which is very easy to look after as it will not crease easily. The colour of its contrast, wadded edge has been carefully selected to co-ordinate with the curtain material.

Another quilted chintz bedcover, with a contrast edge in identical colour and width to the decorative border on the half tester. It is these small details which create a harmonious, professional effect.

the length of your bedcover is the same height above the floor at the sides as it is at the foot end of the bed. There should always be at least 15cm (6in) of bed valance exposed below the bedcover, although this does slightly depend on the drop of the valance. For example, if the bed-base to floor measures approx 33cm (13in), 15cm (6in) is perfect. However, if it is a higher bed, that is with a valance drop of approx 45cm (18in), then the bedcover can stop far higher above the floor: 25cm (10in), perhaps.

Bed size, standard double: 1.88m × 1.35m (6ft 2in × 4ft 6in)
Finished bedcover: 3.2m × 2.36m (10ft 6in × 7ft 9in)

1 Cut two widths 3.29m long (10ft 10in). Cut one of the widths in half lengthways. If the material is patterned you will need to pattern-match the two half-widths on either side of the whole width. As with pelmets, Austrian blinds or round table covers, you must never have a central seam join – it looks dreadful. You must always have the whole width in the middle, with the two half-widths on either side.

2 Follow pattern-matching instructions on page 17.

3 Machine stitch the seams with a 1.5cm (½in) seam allowance. Press to embed the stitches, then press the seam open.

4 Cut lining, approx 10cm (4in) less in total width and length than the actual chintz cover. Deal with it in exactly the same way as with the chintz: i.e. a whole width in the middle with two half-widths on either side. Press the seams open. At what will be the head end of the bedcover, turn over approx 3cm (1¼in). Press and machine stitch. Press again.

5 Cut the interlining the exact same size as the chintz. Cut the two widths, cutting the second one in half lengthways. Take the selvedge of whole width and that of a half-width and overlap them to avoid the bulky ridge of the normal type of seam. Machine stitch with a huge zigzag stitch. Repeat the process for the other half-width.

6 Fold the chintz for the bedcover exactly in half. Draw a curve around the corner of the lower end and cut along the line.

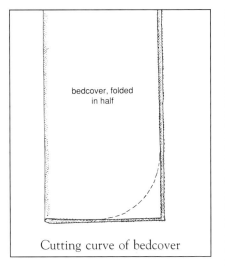

bedcover, folded in half

Cutting curve of bedcover

7 Clamp the interlining on to the table with the top along one end of the table and with one selvedge running lengthways along the very edge of the table.

8 Gently smooth out the interlining. Then manoeuvre the chintz (unfolded, clamping it in place as you position it), right side up, on top of the interlining with its selvedge exactly on top of the interlining selvedge.

9 With the interlining and the material clamped firmly together, fold the material back on itself 30cm (12in) from the clamped selvedge. Ensure that the fold runs straight and parallel to the table edge. The material is now in position (see below) to begin the first line of interlocking stitches 30cm (12in) from the selvedge.

10 Thread a long thin darner needle with a strong thread that matches the chintz. Begin the interlocking stitches 15cm (6in) below the top of the interlining and end the stitching 15cm

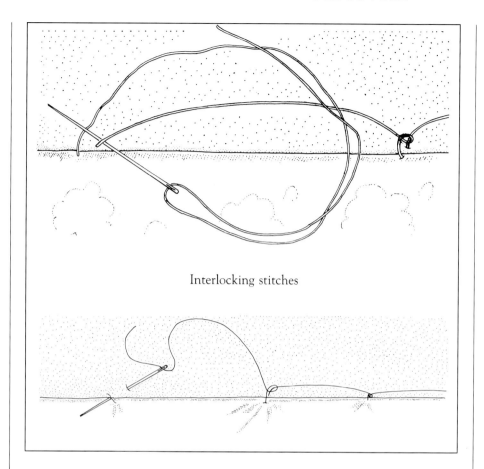

Interlocking stitches

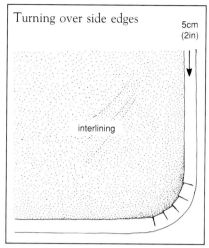

Turning over side edges

5cm (2in)

interlining

(6in) from the bottom of the chintz, so that it will not get in the way of the turnings for hems. First secure the thread to the interlining and a few strands of material at the fold. Then, about 8cm (3in) farther along the fold, insert the needle from front to back through the interlining and then to the front again through the interlining and the chintz. Pick up only a few strands of the chintz with each stitch (see below).

11 To complete the interlocking stitch, pass the needle from bottom to top under the strand between this stitch and the previous stitch, then over the working thread. Pull the thread through to complete the 'interlock', but leaving a slight loop of thread between stitches and not pulling stitches tight (see diagram above). Continue in this way, working an interlocking stitch every 8cm (3in) and leaving slight loops between stitches. The stitches will eventually be hidden in folds of the chintz, so do not worry about their being visible. Unclamp the chintz when you have worked down the length of the table, move it along the table, re-clamp and

continue stitching to within 15cm (6in) of the end of the material.

12 After working the first line of interlocking stitches, starting at the top of the chintz again, smooth more chintz material over the interlining and fold back again 30cm (12in) from the last line of interlocking. Then work the second line of interlocking stitches in the same way. Continue in this way working a line of interlocking stitches down the bedcover about every 30cm (12in) across the width, unclamping and pulling more interlining on to the table as required and working the last line of interlocking stitches about 30cm (12in) from the other edge of the chintz.

13 Once the interlocking has been completed it is advisable to put a few pins through the chintz and interlining along the top and down the seam joins. This ensures that the interlining will stay in place while the bedcover is manoeuvred. Eventually, once the lining has been interlocked in place, the layers will be secure.

14 After the interlining has been interlocked to the chintz, the side

edges of the bedcover can be turned to the wrong side and stitched in place. The interlining and chintz are each turned back and stitched separately. Now that the material is interlined you will have to move it gently and with great respect.

Turn the interlined bedcover right side down on the table, with the interlining facing up and one side edge running along the length of the table edge. Fold 5cm (2in) of the interlining to the wrong side all the way round. Pin the interlining as you go. Shape it to curve round the two bottom corners (see above).

15 Thread a long darner with thread matching the chintz and, beginning 15cm (6in) from the top of the material, stitch along the very edge of the pinned and folded interlining. Repeat the interlocking stitch technique, but 4–5cm (1½–2in) apart this time.

When you are stitching the folded edge of the interlining around the foot ends, you will have to do some careful little tucks in the interlining to take up the excess as you go around the curve. Do all four sides of the bedcover before moving on to the next stage.

16 Turn the chintz over your 5cm (2in) turning of the interlining and clamp down one edge at a time. Apart from when you get to the corners, where again you will have to take little tucks, you do not have to use pins at this stage. (This is the joy of these clamps: they dispense with such fiddly things as pins at so many stages.) Put your hand underneath the edge of the bedcover as you do the stitches, catching down the chintz to the interlining.

These stitches do not come through to the front – they should only go as far as the interlining.

As you stitch, you should have a clamp well to your left and to your right, holding the bedcover's edge tight on the table. By doing this, your hand stitches will acquire their own regular tension since the material being stitched will be well controlled. Without the clamps, the bedcover would be able to shift about. Stitch all four sides of the bedcover like this.

17 Place the lining on the bedcover, while it is lying face down on your work table. Just as in curtain making, you want about a 3cm (1¼in) gap between the edges of the cover and the edges of the lining, on the inside. Start by placing the top edge of the lining (the edge you machine stitched a 3cm (1¼in) hem previously) along the top edge (head end) of the bedcover.

18 Slip stitch the lining down most of one vertical side of the bedcover. (Then you will interlock the lining to the whole cover before going on to stitch around the other three sides.) Stop your stitches about 10cm (4in) clear of the top and the (curved) bottom end, as you can fiddle with them later, after you have finished interlocking.

19 You are now going to interlock the lining to the interlined cover, working vertically from the top to bottom (or bottom to top – it doesn't matter which). Repeat the interlining stitches you have just done for the interlining and chintz. Do these lines of stitches every 30cm (12in). (This is more frequent than in curtain making, due to the fact that a bedcover gets a lot more strain than a curtain: it will be handled, folded and unfolded every day – a very stressful life for a soft furnishing item! A curtain, on the other hand, has a very easy time, gliding across a metal rail every day, suspended by its heading and with no human hands to disturb it.) As you work across the bedcover, interlocking the lining to the rest of the bedcover, check all the time that the machine-stitched top edge remains parallel to the edge of the cover while retaining the 3cm (1¼in) gap.

20 Once you have interlocked the entire cover, you can now stitch the rest of the lining around the remaining three sides. The two curved corners will be a little bit of a fiddle, since you have to do tiny tucks again (as you did with chintz) so that it lies fairly flat as it curves around. Fold and clamp the lining into position, then stitch in between the clamps (see technique, step 16).

BEDCOVER WITH RUCHED EDGE

This is an extremely pretty and eye-catching detail well worth putting on to your bedcover if you feel like it. The size of the ruched edge you actually see on the edge of the bedcover is about 2cm (¾in), but this detail uses up a surprising amount of material.

When you decide to ruche the edge of your bedcover with a contrast strip, there is a part of the bedcover that you make in a slightly different way. Cut your entire bedcover 10cm (4in) less wide and 10cm (4in) less long in total. This is because you are not going to do the usual 5cm (2in) fold-over. There is no need for any of this since by adding the contrast ruched band around four sides of your cover, you are totally binding the edge. Therefore this can be raw since it will be entirely covered when bound.

Bed size, standard double: 1.88m × 1.35m (6ft 2in × 4ft 6in)
Finished bedcover: 3.2m × 2.36m (10ft 6in × 7ft 9in)

1 Cut two widths 3.20m (3½yd) long.

Follow steps **2** and **3**, page 44.

4 Cut lining exactly same size as chintz. Sew it together in the same way and press seams open. (Do not make turn-over at top as with ordinary bedcover.)

Follow steps **5–12**, pages 44–5.

13 Once you have interlocked the interlining to the chintz, pin the two raw edges of the chintz and interlining all the way round.

14 Place the lining on the interlining of the cover. Interlock as in last section but do not sew any edge of the lining at all. Once you have interlocked the lining to the bedcover, pin all four raw edges of the lining to the other raw edges of the interlining and the chintz. Do this by simply moving the existing pins so they include all three parts of the bedcover.

15 Tack, with strong stitches, around all four sides of the bedcover. Stitch 1.5cm (½in) in from the edge. The stitches can go through to the front as they will be covered by the ruched edge.)

Making the ruched band
1 Cut the strips for the ruched edge. You will need 80cm (1yd) contrast material. You then must cut this material in strips 8cm (3in) wide and 11.2m (12¼yd) long in total. Cut on straight grain of material not on the cross (bias).

2 Join strips up. Machine gather on either side for ruching (see page 21), but machine stitch 1cm (¼in) from edge of strip.

3 With raw edges and right sides together, pin the ruched strip to the bedcover around four sides. Machine stitch the strip around the whole cover, with a 1.5cm (½in) seam allowance, taking out the pins as you get to them. Do not press this seam in any way. You do not want to flatten the gathers – you want them to retain their natural bounce.

4 Now fold the ruched band over the raw edge of the bedcover. (Do not trim the seam.) Do this with the bedcover lying right side down on your work table. When you have folded it over to the back of the bedcover, fold under the raw edge of the ruched strip at the second machine-stitching line. Pin this and hand stitch with frequent slip stitches. When you get to the corner you will find the ruched strip will follow the curve with ease as it is so gathered.

The contrast, ruched edge on this bedcover gives it depth and interest, and ties it in neatly with the window pelmet.

6

HEADBOARDS

A headboard for the bed, which matches and tones in with other furnishings, adds a comfortable, luxurious touch to a bedroom. If you would like a special, upholstered headboard in a wonderful shape with details like ruched or pleated piped bands, you must either pay someone a lot of money to make it (using horsehair padding and tacks), or else do a long course to learn the skill yourself which is physically quite tough. Instead, here are instructions to make a padded, buttoned headboard which looks just as professional, and is very easy.

MAKING A HEADBOARD

Here are instructions to make a headboard for a divan-type bed base (check for rubber-cvovered screws at the head end of the bed).

Bed size, standard double: 1.88m × 1.35m (6ft 2in × 4ft 6in)

All you need is the following equipment:

– Timber or blockboard approx 1m (40in) × 1.45m (4ft 10in). Do *not* use chipboard because (a) it is very heavy and therefore hard to manage; and (b) a manual staple gun struggles to fire its staples into it except on the edge
– Two wooden battens 1cm × 4cm (½in × 1½in), 80cm (32in) long (for the legs of the headboard)
– Four screws 3–4cm (1½in) long
– Foam rubber 5cm (2in) thick to cover the area of the headboard
– Evo-stik (impact adhesive) to glue foam rubber on to the timber
– Material and lining to cover the front and the back of the headboard respectively. The front material *must* be cut at least 12cm (5in) bigger than the timber all the way round
– Twelve 22mm (1in) self-cover metal buttons
– Braid to cover edges of headboard (measure when headboard completed)
– Copydex (fabric or wood-working) glue – to attach braid to material of headboard
– Manual staple gun and 8mm (½in) staples

– Long upholstery needle, approx 20cm (8in)
– Heavy thread or fine string (that will fit through eye of a large needle)
– Electric jigsaw and power drill, or friendly handyman who can cut and drill timber for you

1 Make a template, of the shape you want your headboard to be, out of newspaper. Always cut out the template with the newspaper folded in half. If you find it hard to draw a pretty curving shape freehand, piping cord may help you. You can lay it out and move it into different positions until you see the shape you like. Then draw along the line made by the piping cord.

Newspaper template

To check the actual 'look' of the finished headboard it would be wise to hang the newspaper template on the wall, above the bed, using bluetack. This will instantly show you whether the height and width are well balanced with the size of the bed, and other pieces of furniture in the room. Do remember to always try this when the bed is made with all its pillows and the bedcover in place. The presence of these items obviously makes a huge difference to the height and width of the headboard. Maximum height in a headboard makes it look very elegant – the same rule as for pelmets, where length is elegance. So, for example, if the rest of the furniture in the room is rather low (quite likely in a bedroom) and perhaps the window is not very tall either, a tall, elegant headboard can help to right the slight imbalance.

As for width, always cut the timber shape approximately 3cm (1¼in) wider than the bed, at each side. This total of 6cm (2½in) then accommodates the slight extra width in the bed created by a bedcover when it goes over a pair of pillows. If you do not add this extra, the headboard will most likely look skimped in its width.

Once you are happy with your template, lay it on the timber, draw

The detailed, patterned material used here looks best on a plain, rectangular shape. Buttoning gives the headboard an attractive, added depth.

around it and cut it out with an electric jigsaw.

2 Work out, on your paper template, where you would like your buttons to go. The easiest way to do this is to take the actual buttons themselves and lay them on the template in a pattern. Mark the template by making a tiny hole with your pen every time there should be a button. Lay the marked template on the timber and mark the button positions, with a pen, on the timber.

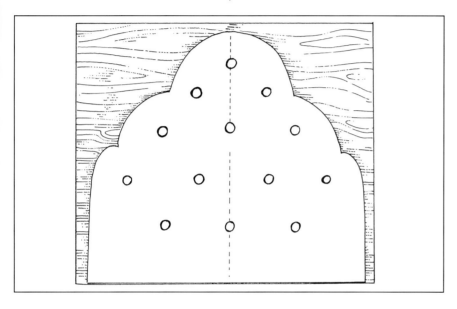

3 Drill a hole no more than 0.5cm (⅛in) large at each pen mark. Bang in two tacks 0.5cm (⅛in) either side of every hole. These are essential to secure the string which will hold the button in place on the other side.

4 Spread Evo-stik, sparingly, over the other side of the headboard and lay on the piece of foam rubber. You may find the thick foam rubber edges very cumbersome around the top edge of the headboard. If you want, you can trim this away. Use either the electric jigsaw or an electric carving knife or, easiest of all, a very sharp kitchen knife. Hold the knife at an angle and remove the sharp right angle of foam rubber. It is not strictly necessary to do this because when you eventually pull the material tightly over the top and anchor it with staples, an undulating curve is naturally formed in the foam rubber and looks perfect.

5 When the glue is dry, take your piece of material and staple it on to the bottom of the headboard at the back. Staple approx every 3cm (1¼in), about 2cm (¾in) in from the edge.

6 Having completed the lower part, do the top next. Start in the centre and work to the left and then the right. This part is slower and more fiddly as you have to take the trouble to get rid of as many rucks as possible as you follow around the gentle curves of your shape. Pull the material particularly tightly here since one of your priorities is to squash down the foam rubber with its sharp right-angled edge.

7 Now move on to one of the sides and continue stapling in the usual way. When you arrive at the bottom corner, mitre it neatly: fold the corner of the material to the back and staple. Then fold the other two sides over it and staple.

8 Now do the last side. You must pull the material extremely tight since it is the last chance you have to take up any slack or get rid of any rucks.

9 Cover the buttons with material.

10 Thread up your upholstery needle with double, very thick thread or else with very thin string. Put a strong knot at the end. Feed the needle through one of the holes in the headboard from the back to the front. Anchor the knot over one of the tacks beside the hole.

Feed the needle through the metal loop at the back of the button. Then feed the needle back through the

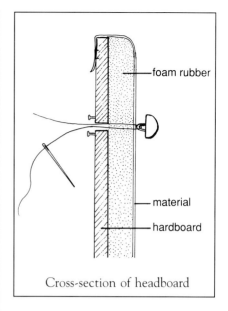

Cross-section of headboard

chintz and foam rubber to the back of the headboard. It is sometimes difficult to find the hole again. You may find that if you poke another long upholstery needle through from the back, you can use it to guide the actual one you are using back through the hole again. However, make sure you leave a 1cm (½in) gap in the material from the first bit of thread.

11 To effectively 'sink' the button, deeply, into the foam rubber (which has such an excellent effect), you need to push the button in with your thumb while you secure the string at the back, on the tacks. It is not enough to merely pull the string or thread hard, hoping the button will sink: the material will most likely rip between the two parts of the string or thread, and it will not be easy to persuade the button to sink properly without the pressure of the thumb.

12 To secure the sunk button effectively, do a figure of eight around the two tacks and then knot the thread well.

Repeat the button instructions for all the remaining buttons.

13 At this point it is worth screwing the legs on to the headboard so that they will eventually be covered by the lining – a particularly neat and professional touch. With an electric jigsaw cut a groove 25cm (10in) long, 0.5cm (¼in) wide up the middle of the batten.

14 Drill two holes in the other half of the batten, one 5cm (2in) from the

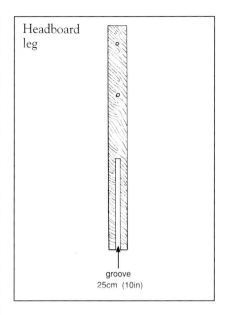

Headboard
leg

groove
25cm (10in)

stage, want to hammer in the tacks either side of the button holes, but this is not entirely necessary – only if you are very much a perfectionist. There is no need to worry about the heads of the tacks scratching your walls because:
– the skirting board around the edge of the room will prevent the back of the headboard touching the wall
– the legs will have the same effect
– the lining will cover the tacks completely.

To staple on the lining along the base of the headboard first turn the bottom edge in, so that the fold of it comes about halfway across the very edge of the timber. Fire the staples very frequently along the fold, about 1–1.5cm (¼–½in) apart. When you get to the timber legs, you will have to cut the lining a little (at a diagonal into the corner where the board meets the leg) and turn it under in the appropriate way.

16 Having stapled all around the four sides of the board, now cover the staples with a pretty braid. The braid can be as wide as the timber or else merely wide enough to cover the staples and a little bit of lining.

Use Copydex (fabric glue) to glue it

down, but it is essential to use it sparingly and not to spill any. Although it is a water-based glue, a yellow/brown mark will appear a few years later. Spread the glue neatly around the sides of the headboard and let it gel, for about 5 minutes, so it will not ooze through braid or out beyond its sides. Feed on braid around four sides, and finish it off neatly at the bottom.

17 You are now ready to screw the headboard on to the bed base. Of course, the useful thing about the nature of the rubber-covered bed-base screws and the timber legs (in which you have cut a slot) is that you can adjust the height of the headboard with ease. It is best to have the bottom of the headboard approximately level with the top of the mattress.

end and the other 30cm (12in) from the first one. Screw these battens onto the back of the headboard to form its legs. The distance apart on the headboard of the legs depends on the location of rubber-covered screws, at the head of your bed base. Remember to check this before screwing on the legs.

15 With the legs of the headboard securely fastened, now line the back of the headboard. You may well, at this

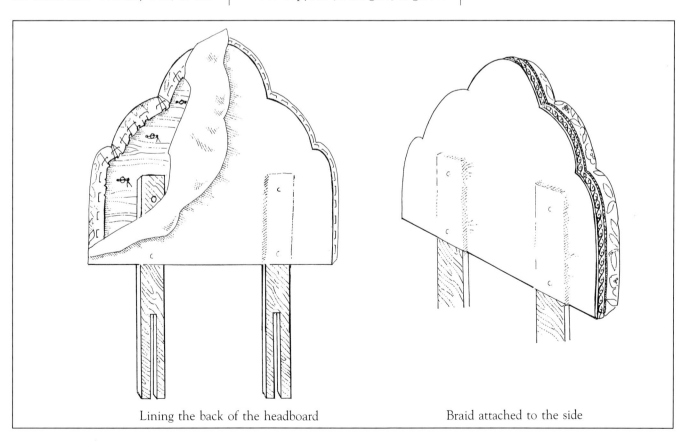

Lining the back of the headboard   Braid attached to the side

7

TABLE COVERS

Covers made from harmonising material can contribute to a bedroom by adding extra decoration, by softening the hard lines of a table, and even by hiding an otherwise unattractive piece of furniture. It is possible to buy round, TV or dressing tables made out of chipboard which, when covered, provide a useful and beautiful table for very little cost.

ROUND TABLE COVERS

The vital key to the success of a table cover is your choice of fabric (see tips below).

The advantage of these tables is that they come in a huge variety of sizes, so you can select any one you want. (See list of suppliers, page 124.) The alternative can be an exhausting search through department stores or antique shops for a small, useful table that fits perfectly, which can also be wildly more expensive.

It is often possible to order one of these tables over the telephone. One UK company (see list of suppliers) will deliver it, to your door, along with the 4mm (¼in)-thick circle of glass for the top (essential to keep your cover clean).

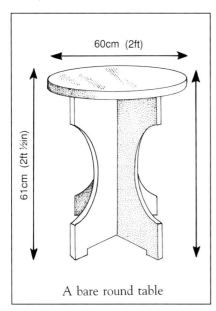

60cm (2ft)

61cm (2ft ½in)

A bare round table

The table usually comes in three parts: a circle, and two other pieces that, when slotted together, form the very effective legs. The instructions that accompany this kit are very easy to follow, so assembly is an extremely easy task.

In the bedroom, you have the perfect excuse to produce a pretty round table cover for a bedside table, that is as feminine and flouncy as you feel like making it. These look gorgeous when they have a detail at the lower edge, such as a frill, contrast bound, and set on so that the added frill has a 2cm (1¾in) stand-up frill. All this will be explained later (page 55). You can make the cover out of any beautiful chintz or cotton that looks good in your particular bedroom.

Contrast square cover

This is a lovely detail to add to your round table cover. Cut and sew a large square of a contrasting material to place over your round table cover, and under the 4mm (¼in) glass. The four corners will fall attractively half-way down the skirt of the cover. It looks good if you accentuate the lines of the square, either by machine stitching some fan edging around its four sides, or by doing some parallel lines of machine embroidery (thick satin stitch, preferably) just in from the edge.

A beautiful alternative is to use antique linen or lace. Or, you can use old embroidered tablecloths, which are not expensive to buy. Don't be put off if they look rather yellow and aged – they wash beautifully. Modern cot-

ton and lace mixtures can also be bought new. Any of these will look good placed on top of a round table with the square points hanging down and the colour underneath showing through the drawn thread-work.

Fringing

Thick bullion fringing, set on the round cover but above its edge so that the actual bullion falls level with the hem of the cloth, is a sumptuous way to finish a round table cover – and it gives the table great presence and strength. (See page 56 for instructions.)

MAKING A ROUND TABLE COVER

Sample table size: 61cm (24in) high × 60cm (23½in) across

1 Measure the table height from floor to its top edge, then across the top and down to the floor again. That measurement is the finished diameter of your table cover. In this case it will be 61cm + 60cm + 61cm (24in + 23½in + 24in).

Therefore quantity of material needed will equal
182cm + 3cm (for seams) × two widths = 3.7m
(6ft + 1in × 2 = 4yd 2in).
Remember to add on pattern repeat, if needed.

Round table covers are both useful and pretty, especially with a set-on frill around the lower edge.

A linen or lace square thrown over a round table cover creates a very attractive but cheap bedside table.

2 Cut two widths of material 1.85m (6ft 1in) long. (This includes seam allowances.)

3 Just as with a bedcover or curtains, put one width in the middle, and cut the other longways up the middle. You may have to pattern-match if you are using patterned material (see page 17). Join the seams; press to embed the stitches; then press open.

4 Fold the cover in half and then in quarter. Get a pen, a piece of string and a drawing pin. Take the diameter of the finished cloth (which you measured in step 1) and divide it by two. Add on 1.5cm (½in) for a seam allowance.

Tie a loop at one end of the string and, using a drawing pin, secure the piece of string on the very edge of the corner of the cover. At this point it is highly advisable to be working on the floor or on a very large wooden table, as you need to be able to prick the pin into something to secure it – even if it is merely a shallow pile carpet.

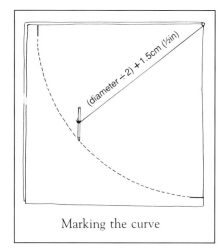

Marking the curve

Now tie the other end of the string to your pen so that when it is swivelled in a curve, in an *exact* vertical position across the material, it will measure exactly the radius, 92.5cm (36½in) from the drawing pin. Having tied your knot securely, swivel your pen in an arc from one side to the other of your folded material. Once you have drawn the arc, adjust it slightly so that the last 5cm (2in) at either end is a straight line. Continuing an upward curve at this point could be potentially disastrous, since when you open up the cover you would find a slight V shape instead of a neat, straight edge.

5 Cut along this line with very sharp scissors. When you get to the two edges, it is *vital* to make absolutely sure that your scissors go completely straight for the last 5cm (2in).

6 Now deal with your lining. Cut two widths in the same way as you did for the material, cutting one down the middle lengthways and doing two seam joins. Press.

7 Fold the lining in half. Place the material, also folded in half, on top of it. Draw around its curved edge. Cut. (It's very useful to use the already-cut piece of material as a template and not repeating the drawing pin and string process again. It would be risky to expect the lining to turn out exactly the same size as the material. Using the already-cut shape as a template is highly reliable and you will then end up with two circles exactly the same size.)

8 Place the two circles, right sides together, on top of each other with all the raw edges exactly together. Pin all the way round. Machine stitch with a 1.5cm (½in) seam allowance – but leaving a 25cm (10in) gap unstitched so you are able to turn the cover right sides out.

9 Press the seam flat to embed the stitches before turning. Trim the seam back to 1cm (¼in). Turn right sides out and press again making sure that the lining does not protrude beyond the edge of the chintz on the right side. Hand stitch the gap to close it, using neat little slip stitches. Press this small section.

DEEP FRILL WITH CONTRAST BINDING

A round table cover looks extremely pretty when there is a set-on frill (see page 21), with a stand-up top, starting about halfway up the side of the cover, and finishing exactly at its hem. In order to make this frill you need to work out the circumference of the cover at exactly the point at which you want to stitch on the frill. A 20cm (8in)-long frill looks wonderful on most sizes of tables.

Circumference measurement

The circumference of 20cm (8in) up from edge of cloth is worked out with the formula: $2 \times \pi \times R$ ($\pi = \frac{22}{7}$, R = radius).

The finished diameter of the cloth equals 182cm. Take away 2×20cm (20cm = length of frill.)

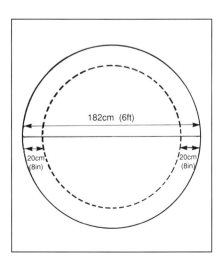

182cm − 40cm = 142cm
R = 142cm ÷ 2 = 71cm
Circumference 20cm up from edge
= $2 \times \frac{22}{7} \times 71$cm
= 446 cm (4.46m)

or in inches:
6ft − (2 × 8in) = 4ft 8in (or 56in)
R = 56in ÷ 2 = 28in
Circumference 8in up from edge
= $2 \times \frac{22}{7} \times 28$in
= 176in (4yd 2ft 8in)

Therefore you need frilling, when finished, to be 446cm (176in) long. For a machine-gathered frill you will need to allow 2½ times the distance of the circumference (but if doing a pleated frill, allow 3 times around).

2½ × 446cm = 1115cm + 3cm (seams) = 1118cm (11.18m)
2½ × 176in = 440in + 1in (seams) = 441in (12¼yd)

Cutting frilling

Cut, on the straight grain of the material:

The contrast binding on this set-on frill both echoes the colour in the bed valance, and adds definition to the round table cover.

11.3m × 20cm (12⅓yd × 8in) each main material and lining.
11.3m × 4cm (12⅓yd × 2in) contrast (twice) for binding top and bottom.

1 Join all widths together vertically, right sides together, with a 1cm (½in) seam allowance. Press open.

2 Join all the lengths, right sides together, horizontally to make a long tube. Turn it right side out and press so that on the right side of the frill there is contrast showing top and bottom. Press.

3 Now machine gather the top of your frill 0.5cm (¼in) below the seam line. Finish the gathering 2cm (¾in) before the end of the long strip. Turn one end in, wrong sides together, 1cm (⅜in).

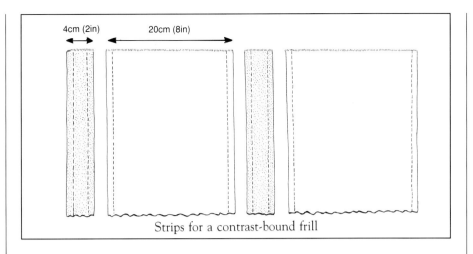

4cm (2in)   20cm (8in)

Strips for a contrast-bound frill

4 Draw a line around the skirt of the table cover 18.5cm (7¼in) above the hem. This is where to attach the frill.

5 Having secured all the gathering, now place the frill on the skirt and pin it exactly on the line which you have drawn around the cover. Machine stitch on, except for the first 5cm (2in). Start with the end you have pressed under.

6 Trim the frill so that there is a small overlap at the ends (1.5cm/½in), then tuck the raw end into the folded end. Slip stitch the remaining frill together and in place.

Adding a fringe

Work out the circumference of the depth of the fringe above the finished length, using $2\pi R$ as previously discussed. Then buy enough fringe to cover this amount. It is hard to join fringe successfully, so it is a nightmare not having enough fringe, but a small excess couldn't matter less.

Interlining round table covers

There is a very easy method of achieving an interlined look to any round table cover. Use an old blanket: most of us have plenty in our cupboards (due to popularity of the duvet instead). Cut the blanket in the exact same circle as the cover but a tiny bit shorter (about 3cm (1½in) all the way round). Before you place the cloth over your round table, first put the blanket on. When your cover is on (and the glass), it looks as if the cover is interlined, but it is merely the blanket. This is all much easier, quicker (and cheaper) than using actual interlining. The effect is the same with the added bonus of making practical use of a formerly redundant blanket. (And it keeps my Scottish blood happy.)

SOLVING PROBLEMS WITH LENGTH

Don't despair if somewhere along the line you have got your calculations a bit wrong and the cover is too long or short for your table. There are things that you can do to solve the problem without involving another stitch.

If cover is too short

There are two alternatives here:

1 You can always use an electric jigsaw. (All husbands ought to own one of these. If he doesn't, give him one for Christmas.) Cut off the necessary measurement from the legs. This would obviously involve disassembling the chipboard table, so that the legs can be clamped on a work bench (another Christmas present) where it can be cut.

2 Using your jigsaw, reduce the diameter of the round table. By doing this, your cloth will then be able to drop lower. You can do this with the table fully assembled. Using this method depends on whether you have already had the glass made, or not.

If cover is too long

Two alternatives:

1 You can make four square blocks to place under the table legs. Do not make the blocks too small. You do not want the legs to slip off these blocks – hence their size: 12cm × 12cm (5in × 5in), and whatever thickness you re-

quire is ideal. Cut a little groove in each block to stop the table legs slipping out.

2 You can have another table top cut. Either chat up your local DIY shop or timber merchant, or else I am sure your supplier would help you – see list of suppliers, page 124. You obviously work out what increased size this second table top needs to be in order to lift your cover sufficiently off the ground so that the hem rests on the carpet or floor boards. Again, this is assuming that you have not had the glass cut as yet. (Even if you have, never mind, just have another one cut. It is not wildly expensive and anything is better than having to re-sew a soft furnishing item.)

Extra tips

I would strongly advise against two things involving round table covers.

1 Do not deliberately cut them much too long. They simply hang badly.

2 I would advise against ever doing a rolled, wadded, or ruched edge along the hem. Although the idea is fun in principle, in practice, it causes the cover to hang extremely badly, since its edge automatically becomes slightly stiff and it takes on its own character which is hard for you to control and arrange as you would like.

TV-TABLE COVERS

It is possible to buy these wonderful tables especially designed to store, out of sight, both a TV and a video (see list of suppliers, page 124.) This table

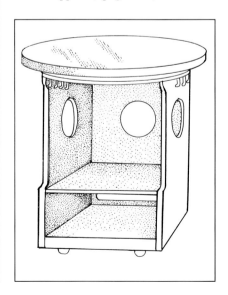

An alternative to a frilled top on a TV table cover is this plain, braided band. The set-on fringe adds weight and echoes the colours in the braid.

is usually accompanied by all the relevant assembling instructions and the 4mm (¼in) circle of glass. I definitely think that hiding such an aesthetic eyesore as a TV is a priority, whether it is in a bedroom, drawing room, study, or playroom.

The great secret in making this object an acceptable piece of furniture, especially in a bedroom, is to make its cover out of very positive and elegant fabric. Certainly in reception rooms, this will remove from resembling anything faintly related to a dressing table. I think the bedroom is the only place in which a pretty chintz cover is acceptable.

The table comes equipped with a curtain rail running around the underside of the circle of chipboard. So now you have to plan to make one continuous curtain to run all the way around, and a top to cover the table top with a pleated frill hanging down at least 12cm (5in).

MAKING A TV-TABLE COVER

Sample TV-table size: 72.5cm (29in) high × 65cm (26in) across

Material needed: 5.10m (5⅔yd); or 6.20m (6¾yd) for alternative frill

Lining: 3.30m (3⅔yd); or 2.60m (3yd) for alternative frill

Curtain hooks: 25 brass hooks

Pleated frilled top

1 Using the chipboard top as a template, cut, out of the main material, a circle of the exact same size plus a seam allowance of 1.5cm (½in) all the way round.

2 Now use the material template to cut out the lining for the circle.

3 Measure the circumference of your table top with a tape measure. In this case it will be approximately 205cm (82in).

4 For pleats, multiply the circumference by 3:
205cm × 3 = 615cm (6.15m)
82in × 3 = 246in (6yd 2ft 6in)

5 Cut out strips 6.25m × 18cm (7yd × 7in). Cut the lining the same length, but 12cm (5in) wide. At this point you can make a decision, which is economical on time but extravagant on money: instead of lining this frill, you can merely cut the material double the length so that when folded in half, wrong sides together, you would then get main material on both sides. This is a terrific time saver in many ways: you do not have to cut out strips of lining, nor machine join them at the hem. However, you want to bear in mind that if your material is bulky, the pleated frill may stick out too much. However, the idea of doing a pleated frill here, and not a gathered one, should help the frill look less flouncy (especially if you press it well once the cover is finished). If using just material for the frill, cut one length 6.25m × 28cm (7yd × 11in), and see steps 8a and 8b.

6 If lining the frill with ordinary lining, machine up and press all the pieces of main material to form one long strip. Then do the same to the lining.

7 With right sides of frill together, place raw edges of main material and lining together. Machine along with a 1cm (½in) seam allowance. (Keep it nice and small, so there will be no need to trim back later – another time saver.) Fold in one (short) end 1.5cm (½in), wrong sides together. Press.

8 Turn up lining, so that wrong sides are together of main material and lining and their two raw edges are level. You should now have achieved an automatic 3cm (1½in) turn-up on the wrong side. Machine stitch raw edges together. Press. (Now go to step **9**.)

8a Machine stitch together all the strips. Press open the seams. Fold in one (short) end 1.5cm (½in), wrong sides together. Press.

8b Fold strip of chintz longways, wrong sides together, so that the raw edges are level. Machine stitch raw edges together with a 1.5cm (½in) seam allowance. Press, especially the fold, so it makes a sharp line.

9 Whether you have used the first or second method to create your frill, you must now follow the pleating-up instructions. (See page 20.)

10 Feed the pleated-up frill on to the table cover circle. Feed it on right sides together, with raw edges level and with a 1.5cm (½in) seam allowance. If you are a little bit nervous you can always pin it on first, but there is honestly no need. When you do attach this pleated frill to the circle, always start with the end you originally turned in and pressed (but did not stitch). Also do *not* stitch the first 5cm (2in) of frill to the material circle. That has to be done later.

11 Once you have stitched around nearly the whole circle – but leave the last 5cm (2in) unstitched – you can then slip in the raw end of the frill inside the folded (but unstitched) other end of the frill. This is an extremely professional way of finishing this off; so neat and tidy – with no raw edges exposed or seams to oversew. Having slipped one end of the frill inside the other, then machine stitch the remaining part of the frill on to the circle. Then slip stitch this part of the frill to hold it in place.

12 You now need to line the circle. Fold all your frill into the middle of the right side of the material circle and

ABOVE *A delicate treatment for a dressing table, using a pleated top with a small stand-up.*

RIGHT *Just as pretty as a kidney-shaped dressing table is this rectangular table, cleverly edged with an attractive border.*

pin every now and again, so that it will stay roughly in place and not get caught up in the next stage you are about to do. Pin the lining circle, right sides together, on to the main material circle around the raw edges. Machine stitch on the material side, so you have a line of stitching to follow but leave a 25cm (10in) gap so that you can then turn the cover right sides out again. But before you turn it, trim the seam back to 0.5cm (¼in). You want to remove all possible bulk here but when you get to the section left open stop trimming the seam. It is a lot easier when you come to turn in, press and hand sew this section, if you still have the full 1.5cm (½in) seam allowance.

13 Having turned the cover, press extremely well (always from the back if possible – I'm always terrified of singeing material with an overheated iron!) Hand sew the 25cm (10in) gap that you left open. The cover is now ready to place on the top of your assembled table, under the glass. But now make and hang your curtain first: it is easier to hang it on its rail without the frill in the way.

TV-table curtain

You only need to make one of these as it starts at the front and goes all the way round the table's circumference. You do not need to interline it. (The quantities given below allow for 2 times around the table.)

1 Cut 3 or 4 widths of material 77.5cm (30½in) long. (Cut 3 widths of 140cm (56in) wide material; 4 widths of 120cm (48in) material.) Allow extra for a pattern-match if necessary. Then follow pattern-matching instructions (page 17).

2 Cut 3 or 4 widths of lining 66.5cm (26in) long. Machine stitch together all the widths. Open seams and press.

3 Put the two lengths of curtain together, with right sides together, and machine stitch along hem edge with 1cm (½in) seam allowance. Start and stop machine stitches 10cm (4in) in from either end.

4 Turn your curtain, so lining and material are wrong sides together and you have created a 5cm (2in) turn-up for the hem. Press a sharp line at the fold.

5 Turn in 5cm (2in) of the main material at each side. Pin. Do a beautiful right-angle fold at the two hem corners. (See steps **6** and **7** page 72, but you do not need lead weights with this particular curtain.)

6 Fold the lining over vertical turnings of curtain leaving a 3cm (1¼in) gap

between the edge of the fold of the main material and the fold of the lining. Slip stitch, not coming through to the front. Press.

7 Turn the top down 3cm (1¼in), using a small ruler to guide you. Pin vertically with pinheads uppermost. Press. At the two corners, fold a neat right-angle corner again. Machine stitch narrow gathering tape on to the top of the curtain, on the wrong side, so that its top is 1cm (½in) below the top of the curtain. It should be easy to line this up so that the lower edge of the tape just covers the raw edge of the material.

You may want to pin the tape on first but there is no need if you are feeling brave. In addition, you may want to draw a pen line 3cm (1¼in) below the top of the curtain to guide you as you machine stitch it on but there is basically no need to do this since the lower raw edge of the material is an excellent guide.

8 Having machined on the tape, pull it up so the curtain measures 2.04m (6ft 10in) at its top. Place a hook every 8cm (3in).

PLAIN TV-TABLE COVER

If you like, you need not make any of the two previous fitted TV-table covers. Instead, you can make an ordinary round table cover (see page 52). Then, when you want to watch TV, you merely pick up and throw its front section over the table top.

As far as covering a TV table, this method is far less contrived and frilly than the two previous methods. However, when you throw a large part of the cover on to the surface of the table, you will disturb things on the table and possibly knock them over.

DRESSING TABLES

Kidney-shaped dressing tables, with a variety of shelves underneath, are also available from the supplier who sells round and TV tables.

You can cover these in exactly the same way as a TV table (see page 57): merely cut the top in the required kidney shape, as opposed to a circle.

It is also possible to cover any sort of rectangular table in the same way.

8

CURTAINS

Although there are many elements of successful bedroom furnishing, from bed valances to dressing table covers, to me the window is the most important thing in the room. Everything about it is a huge influence on the atmosphere you are creating. The 'face' (the window) and its 'crown' or 'hat' (the pelmet) essentially gives the room that special feeling.

CURTAIN DESIGN

It is fun to wear beautiful clothes: they make you feel good. In the same way, stunning window treatments that are absolutely correct in every detail and proportion, are just as satisfying. When I think of windows as being like a face it is vital, for the success of the room, that the face is shown off in the most flattering way possible

When deciding how to dress your window, always remember the basic reasons for curtains.

Decoration: the top priority for curtaining any window is to make it look beautiful, elegant, pretty or dramatic – within the room as a whole.

Softening the lines: the shape of a window is usually hard, and not very beautiful, unless you live in a historic house. Curtains soften the very straight lines of window architraves.

Insulation: being able to draw curtains at night makes a huge difference to room temperature, as they add extra layers of insulation. This is one good reason for ensuring that there are no radiators under your windows – otherwise it is very easy for heat to go straight up the curtains without heating the room.

Privacy: curtains or blinds prevent people being able to see in at night, and so give a wonderful feeling of security.

Softening sound: thick, interlined curtains help to soak up the noise in a room. You will notice a marked difference between the noise level in the room before and after it is curtained.

So, keeping all these vital considerations in mind, now set out to design the perfect window treatment for your particular bedroom.

Curtain length

Always remember that the longer you can make a pelmet or curtain design for a bedroom, the more elegant the window, and the room, will look.

I prefer my curtains to come to the floor and brush it, but no more. Avoid short curtains at all costs. If you have a problem with a radiator under a window, consider an Austrian blind instead (see page 118), framed with a pair of long dress curtains.

In some instances adding an extra 15cm (6in) on to full-length curtains can look very lavish and full. But there are four great disadvantages to these extra-long curtains: the curtains do not hang as well; you have to take trouble to dress, or arrange, them every day; pets come and lie on them; and it is hard to run the vacuum around them. However, if they are never to be closed, this extra length looks sensational.

Drop for curtains with pelmets

Measuring the 'drop' or length of your curtains is the first thing you need to do when determining the amount of curtain material you will need. If you are using a pelmet to crown your curtains, the curtains will begin at the underside of the *pelmet board*. This is a flat piece of wood which juts out into the room from the wall. It holds the curtain rail, and the pelmet is hung from its edge.

Pelmet positions

To determine the drop of your curtains, you must first decide on the position of the board. If the board is already in place, and you are happy with its position, then you can measure from this board. But make sure that the board is *securely* fastened to the wall.

The obvious place for the pelmet board is sitting horizontally on the top of the window architrave (or frame). However, if you want to add height to the window shape you can position the board higher above the architrave, thus gaining as much extra height as you like. The space between the top of the architrave and the bottom of the pelmet board is called 'dead wall', since it is the wall that will eventually be permanently hidden behind the pelmet. By raising the pelmet board above the window frame you will have 'raised' the height of the window and made it look taller and narrower than it actually is. Visually you are 'raising' the height of the ceiling. The optimum distance for this is 5–15cm (2–6in) and certainly not more than 20cm (8in). It doesn't matter how much space there is between the pelmet and the ceiling. If necessary you can screw straight into the ceiling.

There are three possible reasons for raising the pelmet board:

– To enable you to create a deep pelmet
– To minimize loss of light
– To make a low ceiling appear higher.

You may wish to create the deepest pelmet possible, while retaining the

balance between curtain and pelmet, and between window treatment and room, with a view to maximum elegance. Minimising the loss of light from the window is also worth keeping in mind, especially if the window is north- or east-facing. Lastly, 'raising' a low ceiling will help to create the illusion of more space in your room.

Once you have decided on the position of your pelmet board, you should make sure that you will be able to fix the correct size of board to the wall in this position.

FIXING PELMET BOARD AND RAILS

Making and fixing a pelmet board and curtain rail is, of course, a job for a carpenter or skilled handyman. However, the instructions are given here in detail because they are an important

Two different lengths of curtains are used in this pleasant, restful room due to the window seat. Short curtains clear the window seat in the middle, but dress curtains on either side, together with the gathered seat valance, suggest that all the curtains are elegantly long.

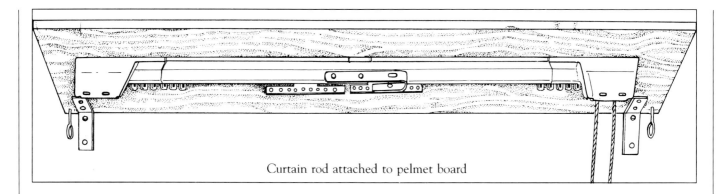

Curtain rod attached to pelmet board

part of achieving a successful curtain design.

Especially when attaching the pelmet board to the wall, not using a skilled person is a false economy. The pelmet board needs to be strong enough to hold the weight of great lengths of lined and interlined material. It may not be apparent to an amateur how to fix the pelmet successfully to the wall above the window, and damage can inadvertently be done to the wall.

Size of pelmet board
The pelmet board should almost always be 17cm (6¾in) deep and 2cm (¾in) thick. When purchasing the board at a timber (lumber) yard, you should ask for '7in by 1in' board. If you actually measure it you will find it is closer to 6¾in by ¾in. This is because once a '7 by 1' has been planed it is no longer quite as wide or as thick as its name implies.

The curtain rail is fixed lengthwise to the centre of the board, ending about 2cm (¾in) from each end.

I only use a narrower board where the room and window treatment are quite small and where I therefore would not want a deep pelmet board jutting out into the room – it would look too cumbersome and heavy. In this case a board no narrower than 10cm to 12.5cm (4in to 5in) would be used.

The width of the board is determined by the width of the window treatment. It should extend past the window the width required for the housing space on either side (see Table 3 on page 66).

Curtain-housing space
Next, you must add on housing space (US: 'stackback') for the curtains on either side of the window. (See page 65.)

A certain amount of wall space on either side of the window needs to be available to accommodate, or 'house', the curtains when they are drawn fully open. The curtains must hang clear of the window when they are open, so that they do not reduce any of the light coming into the room.

Fascia and vertical returns
If you are hanging a pelmet that has a fusible buckram band at its top (see page 81), you will need a strong plywood fascia along the front of the board for support and vertical timber returns. (In American terminology you will need a 'cornice board'.) The plywood fascia is fixed to the front of the standard-sized pelmet board, and the vertical timber returns (or sides) must be screwed into the ends of the board (see below). The buckram-faced pelmet is stretched across the fascia and around the sharp corners.

The vertical returns should be made in the same '7 by 1' timber as the pel-

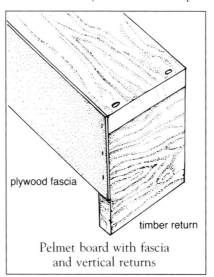

plywood fascia

timber return

Pelmet board with fascia and vertical returns

met board and will therefore measure 17cm (6¾in) square and 2cm (¾in) thick.

The fascia should be made of 3mm (⅛in)-thick strong plywood. If the pelmet will have a fusible buckram band at its top, cut the plywood so that it is just slightly longer, vertically, than the buckram. For example, if the band is 12cm (4¾in) deep, use a plywood fascia about 14cm (5½in) deep. This fascia gives terrific support to the pelmet and makes it look very professional especially because you can then achieve sharp corners. Therefore I advise using a plywood fascia for goblet-pleated pelmets (page 83), deep smocking (page 88) and deep pencil-pleated pelmets (page 82).

Curtain rails
A good-quality curtain rail with a pulley system (in American terminology a 'traverse rod') is essential (see suppliers list, page 124). The curtains will be opened and closed countless times, and a good rail and pulley system will work smoothly for a long time.

Rails come in various types. You can get ones that are 'telescopic', which pull and push to differing sizes. Good curtain-rail manufacturers will also make made-to-measure rails, heavy-duty or regular, made to your own specifications. They will even make special rails to curve around a bay window if necessary.

Look for rails that have very clear instructions for attaching them. When using a pelmet board, you will want a rail that has a 'top fix' so that it

The contrast leading edge on these curtains adds an extra detail which ties in with the pelmets, and adds a little extra definition to the room.

can be screwed to the board above it. A good metal rail will have clear instructions on how to load and unload the runners and centralise the overlap arm.

Attaching the curtain rod

The rail *must* be attached to the pelmet board rather than to the wall. Timber is far stronger and more reliable than plaster. Once the rail is on the board, the board is screwed firmly to the wall. The weight of the curtains will then be evenly distributed along the rail. More importantly, the stress of the pulley system, at one end of the rail, will be well accommodated in the timber and not at one pressure point in the plaster.

The rail should be set halfway back from the front of the board (see page 62). This is essential so that full curtains, as they are drawn backwards and forwards, will not in any way disturb beautifully dressed pelmets. Hence the necessity of pelmet boards no less than 17cm (6¾in) wide.

Brackets and screws

The brackets are attached to the pelmet board at either end (see page 62). A central bracket is advisable if the board is over about 1.40m (4ft 7in).

Use very tough, strong brackets about 5cm by 8cm (2in by 3in). Securely attach each bracket into the timber board with two screws.

Screw eyes on pelmet board

Because you are top-fixing the rail and not using the wall brackets provided with the rail, you do lose one advantage; this is the use of the special holes

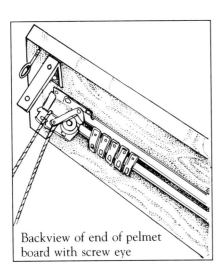

Backview of end of pelmet board with screw eye

in the wall brackets, which would enable you to turn a right angle with your curtain to meet the wall. Instead, you have to create your own system for the curtain to reach the wall. This is easily done. Merely place a large screw eye, about 3cm (1¼in) long, at both back corners of the board.

The last curtain hook is hooked into this screw eye, thereby turning the end of the curtain into the wall.

Fixing pelmet board to wall

The screws that attach each bracket to the wall should be at least 3cm (1¼in) long. Rawl plugs need to be inserted into the holes in the wall, and the pelmet board should be fixed in a level position using a spirit level. It is highly recommended that you hire a professional to attach your pelmet board. It is not worth risking damaging your wall or having your curtains fall down.

The pulley system

You must, if you possibly can, employ a pulley system. It is essential that your hands, however clean, do not yank the curtains twice a day. The leading edges at the centre will get dirty, and the dirt, along with the effects of the sun, will eventually cause the fabric to rot.

There are two choices you have for a pulley system. One choice is to use the plastic tensioner in the curtain-rail kit. It is screwed into the skirting board (U.S. 'baseboard') near the floor or into the wall. The continuous nylon cord is looped on to the sprung tensioner. The cord is then shortened from the centre at the overlap arm (see overlap arm on rail on page 62) until it is tight.

Complete instructions for setting up the system are provided with the curtain rod.

The second choice you have for your pulley system is one I prefer. I use a pair of brass acorns in place of the plastic tensioner.

First you should follow the curtain-rod instructions to centralise the overlap arm.

You then cut the cord to the desired length and thread the two cord ends through a tiny S-hook 1.5cm (½in) long to prevent them from twisting. After this, thread each end through a brass acorn.

However, if your window is very wide and not very tall – for example,

3.5m (11½ft) wide and 2.15m (7ft) tall – then you have to use the plastic tensioner.

This will allow the continuous cord, within the rail, to draw the curtains backwards and forwards. If you were to cut the cord to put brass acorns on, you would not be able to draw the curtains backwards and forwards without having a large length of cord lying on the floor.

Measuring the drop

1 You can easily determine your finished drop *before* your pelmet board is in place. Decide where the bottom of the board will sit, and measure from that position.

Unfold your long folding ruler and hold it fully extended up against the window frame, at one side of the window, with the end of the ruler which is marked with 2m (6ft) resting on the floor. Make a faint mark with a soft pencil on the window frame at the top of the ruler.

2 Then move the extended ruler up until the top of it just reaches the point where the bottom of the pelmet board will be, either at the top of the window frame or a short distance above it as desired.

3 Add together the two measurements just obtained to determine the total measurement between the floor and the bottom of the pelmet board.

In order to determine the curtain drop from this figure you must subtract 3cm (1¼in) – of which 2cm (¾in) is for the drop of the curtain rail and its runners and 1cm (½in) is for unlaid carpet (assuming the carpet has a shallow pile). If the carpet is already in place, subtract only the 2cm (¾in) to accommodate the curtain rail and the runners at the top.

Window clearance

The next step in measuring your window, after the curtain drop has been calculated, is to measure the window width. But first, always check for anything that will obstruct the clearance around the window, such as a boxed-in radiator, an adjacent wall or a ceiling beam.

You must take these obstructions into consideration and adjust your width measurements accordingly. Whatever happens, the whole curtain and pelmet design must be absolutely

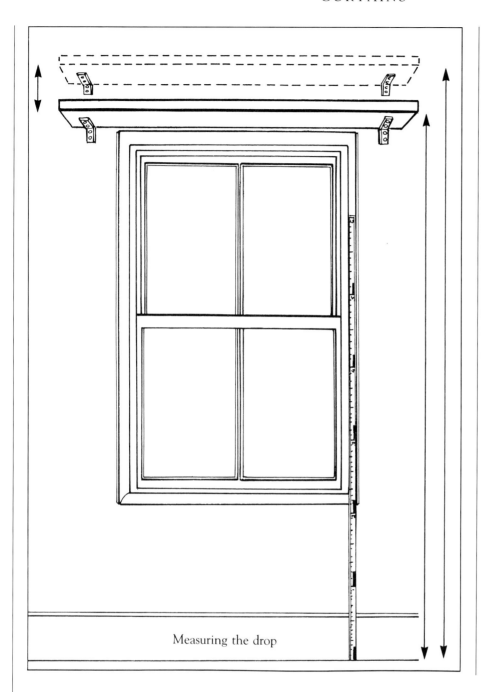

Measuring the drop

ing the width of the window is the first step in determining both the width of the pelmet board and the width of each finished flat curtain.

Curtain housing space

Don't forget to add on curtain housing space (stackback), on each side of the window.

Table 1 (below) indicates approximately how much empty wall space will be needed on either side of the window (outside the frame) to house the curtains on different window widths. The housing space given for each window width will be the approximate amount necessary to clear the curtains off the window. Thus, to determine the size of the pelmet board, add the width of the window and that of the housing space on either side of the window (see page 62).

Curtain material widths

As a general rule each finished curtain, when flat, should measure not less than 2⅓ times the width it must cover (including the housing space and the extra width allowance) (see page 66) and not more than 2½ times the width.

Table 2 (page 66) gives the approximate number of widths (selvedge to selvedge) of curtain material that should be used for each curtain for a given window width. This table is for quick reference only.

If you are using material of a different width, use the 2⅓–2½ times rule above to calculate the width of your finished curtain.

When deciding how many material widths you need, do not cut widths

symmetrical with the window itself. Otherwise the curtains will draw together off-centre. Also, the pelmet board must be absolutely level (not necessarily with the top of the window which may be slightly tilted – especially in an old house). This can be determined with the aid of a spirit level.

Measuring window width

The window width is measured from outer edge to edge of the vertical parts of the architrave, or window frame, on either side of the window. Determin-

TABLE 1	
Housing space required for a window	
Window width*	Housing space each side of window
50cm (1ft 8in)	5cm (2in)
80cm (2ft 8in)	7cm (2¾in)
1.25m (4ft 1in)	10cm (4in)
1.60m (5ft 3in)	15cm (6in)
1.90m (6ft 3in)	15cm (6in)
2.40m (7ft 11in)	20cm (8in)
2.80m (9ft 2in)	25cm (10in)
3.30m (10ft 10in)	30cm (12in)
3.80m (12ft 6in)	30cm (12in)

*Window width is measured from edge of architrave to edge of architrave.

TABLE 2
Approximate number of curtain widths required for a window

The number of widths given here is approximate and is based on a 137cm (54in)-wide curtain material, interlined with a medium-weight interlining.
Note: This guide is for a quick reference only and TABLE 5 should be read before purchasing material.

Window width	No. widths in each curtain
50cm (1ft 8in)	½ width
80cm (2ft 8in)	1
1.25m (4ft 1in)	1½
1.60m (5ft 3in)	2
1.90m (6ft 3in)	2
2.40m (7ft 11in)	2½
2.80m (9ft 2in)	3
3.30m (10ft 10in)	3½
3.80m (12ft 6in)	4

less than one-half the width of the material. The difference a narrower width makes is not worth the effort, so if in doubt, always go for a slightly wider curtain. Remember that 2½ times the width is an *approximate* aim. If it works out at only 2 times the width don't worry. By the time it is finished and beautifully dressed into its folds, it will look wonderful.

The next section describes in detail how to calculate the width each finished pleated curtain must cover once it is hanging.

DETERMINING FABRIC AMOUNTS

Now you can begin the process of determining the amount of curtain material that you will need for your particular curtain design.

Curtain and pelmet-board widths
Tables 3 and 4 give an example of how you should make your calculations. They establish a hypothetical or sample window and show clearly how to work out the pelmet-board width and the finished curtain width. As you can see from **Table 3**, the pelmet-board width is determined by adding the housing space required (see **Table 1**) to the window width measured between the outer edges of the window architrave.

Extra width allowance
For curtains with a pelmet you must add an extra 10cm (4in) to each curtain to accommodate the overlap arm

(U.S. 'master slide') on the curtain rail, and the fact that the curtains turn into the wall at the sides. The ends of the pelmet board are called the 'pelmet-board returns'.

It is essential that the ends of your curtains do meet the wall at the sides, because a gap looks very unappealing and because you want to stop all draughts coming from the window.

The extra width allowance of 10cm (4in) is calculated on the basis of a rail that has a 5cm (2in) overlap at the centre and a pelmet-board 17cm (6¾in) deep.

Finished width of pleated curtain
Of course, each curtain will have to extend across half of the pelmet board once it has been pleated. But the *extra width allowance* must also be added to each curtain to cover the overlap arm and the curtain turning into the wall – called the 'return'.

TABLE 3
Determining width of pelmet board for sample window

This is an example of how to calculate the width of your pelmet board.

First measure:

Window width (architrave to architrave)	1.60m (5ft 3in)

Then determine *housing space* by referring to TABLE 1 (page 65):

Total housing space (on both sides of window)	15cm (6in) × 2 = 30cm (12in/1ft)

To determine the pelmet board width simply add the *window width* and the *total housing space*:

Window width	1.60m (5ft 3in)
Total housing space	+ 30cm (1ft)
Pelmet board width	**1.90m (6ft 3in)**

TABLE 4
Determining finished width of each sample curtain heading after pleating

This is an example of how to determine the *finished width* of each of the two curtains across the heading after pleating.

First calculate the measurement of *one half of the pelmet board width* (see TABLE 2):

Pelmet board width	1.90m	(6ft 3in)
1.90m (6ft 3in) ÷ 2 =	95cm	(3ft 1½in)
One half of pelmet board width	95cm	(3ft 1½in)

Then add half the *pelmet board width* and the *extra width allowance* (for the overlap arm at the centre of the rail and for the pelmet board return):

One half of pelmet board width	95cm	(3ft 1½in)
Extra width allowance	+ 10cm	(4in)
Finished width of curtain after pleating	**1.05m**	**(3ft 5½in)**

When you are gathering your curtain up on heading tape or pleating your curtain, this total width of each finished pleated curtain is the width you are aiming for (see **Table 4**).

This is also the width that you must multiply by 2½ to estimate how wide the finished flat curtain must be (before it is gathered or pleated) (see Curtain material widths page 65).

Calculating material quantity

Table 5 illustrates how to calculate the required material for the sample window in **Table 3**. After you have determined the necessary curtain drop as well as the number of fabric widths needed for each curtain, you are ready to calculate the amount of curtain material you will need to purchase.

This calculation is, of course, a very important one, as a mistake can be very expensive. So do not rush the process. Take as much time as you need, first to measure your windows and then to make calculations. Check your calculations (and measurements, for that matter) at least twice.

Extra drop allowances

As you can see from **Table 5**, to calculate the total length to allow for each unsewn drop of curtain material you must add allowances for the following:

– Hem at bottom of curtain
– Turn-down at top of curtain
– Pattern repeat

Generally 12cm (4¾in) is the measurement for hemming on all lined curtains. The turn-down at the top of the curtain will vary according to the type of heading you have chosen. The sample curtain has a turn-down allowance at the top of 8cm (3¼in) which is enough for a pencil pleat (U.S. 'shirred') heading.

Pattern repeats

The excess amount allowed for the pattern repeat also varies from one material to another. A totally plain fabric, of course, will not need an allowance added for pattern repeats. But for all printed materials and even

A single pair of curtains has been used here to cover both windows and door in a single sweep. Plain, buckram tie-backs hold back the curtains to allow in extra light.

TABLE 5
Calculating curtain material needed for sample window

This is an example of how to calculate the quantity of material needed for the curtains for the sample window in TABLE 3 (not including the pelmet fabric). The hypothetical curtain material has a pattern repeat of 33cm (13in), and the curtains will have a *pencil-pleat* (U.S. 'shirred') *heading*.

Note: The *turn-down* allowance at the top of the curtain is determined by the type of heading chosen.

First calculate the unsewn drop or 'cutting length' of each width by adding curtain drop, hem and turn-down at top:

1) Curtain drop	2.80m	(9ft 2½in)
2) Hem at bottom of curtain	12cm	(4¾in)
3) Turn-down* at top	8cm	(3in)
Cutting length	**3.00m**	**(9ft 10¼in)**

Now add the length of the pattern repeat to calculate the drop allowance needed:

1) Cutting length	3.00m	(9ft 10¼in)
2) Pattern repeat	33cm	(13in)
Each drop allowance measures	**3.33m**	**(10ft 11¼in)**

Then decide how many widths you need altogether for both curtains (see TABLE 2) and multiply this by the *drop allowance*:

Drop allowance	3.33m	(10ft 11¼in)
No. of widths = 4		
(2 widths for each curtain)	×4	
	13.32m	(43ft 9in)
You will need to purchase	**13.5m (15yd) of material**	

---

for some textured patterns, you should always measure the length of each pattern repeat.

Pattern-matching is not difficult so long as you have allowed sufficient excess for each drop. You will need to add on one pattern repeat for every drop of material (see **Table 5** above for an example of how to add on the pattern repeat allowance).

See page 17 for instructions on pattern-matching.

Lining and interlining amounts

The lining and interlining are always the same width as the curtains. But because there is no need for pattern-matching, you will probably need less material.

You must take into account the width from selvedge to selvedge of the lining and interlining. This may not match the width of the curtain material. Whatever the fabric width, the joined widths must cover the same distance as the joined curtain material widths.

Pelmet material amounts

If you are making a pelmet, you should add the amount for your pelmet into your total calculation for material. The instructions for calculating this are given on page 82.

It may not be necessary to add on for frills (see pages 18–21), as you may have enough material left over from the excess added for pattern repeats. However, do calculate carefully the total amount needed for frills.

MAKING CURTAINS

To take you as clearly as possible through the step-by-step process of making a pair of simple lined and interlined pencil-pleated curtains, I will use sample curtains. The dimensions of these are the same as used in **Tables 1, 3** and **4** and are as follows:

– Finished drop 2.80m (9ft 2½in)
– Cutting length 3.00m (9ft 10¼in)
– Two widths for each curtain

The pencil-pleat heading has been chosen for the sample curtains because it is the heading that is both the simplest to make and the best heading for curtains with a pelmet.

TABLE 6
Measurements of sample curtain with pencil-pleat heading

This diagram shows how the unsewn curtain looks once the curtain widths have been joined, but before the interlining, hemming and lining have begun.

a Finished curtain drop	2.80m	(9ft 2½in)
b Hem at bottom of curtain	12cm	(4¾in)
c Turn-down at top	8cm	(3¼in)
d Cutting length	3.00m	(9ft 10½in)
e One width (selvedge to selvedge)	137cm	(54in)
f Turn-back at edges	5cm	(2in)
g Approximate finished flat curtain width:		
(137 × 2) – (2 × 5) – 4 (selvedges)	2.60m	(8ft 6½in)

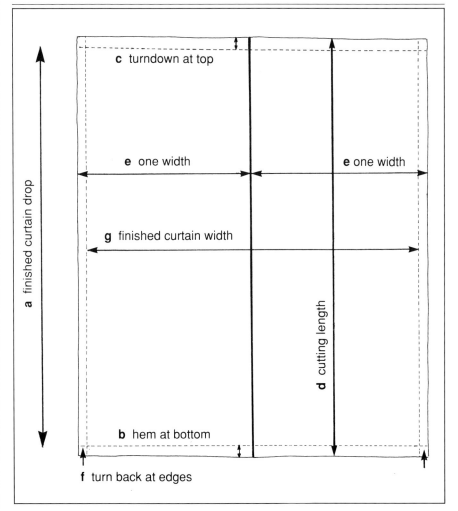

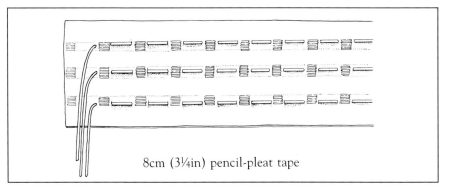

8cm (3¼in) pencil-pleat tape

The cutting length
The cutting length for each width of curtain material is always determined by adding to the desired finished curtain drop the allowance for the hem at the bottom and the turn-down at the top (see **Table 5** on page 67).

In the case of our sample curtains we are adding 8cm (3in) for the turn-down at the top of the curtain, which is sufficient for a pencil-pleat heading. The turn-down is not the same for every type of heading, so make sure you know exactly what is required for the type of heading you have chosen.

Heavy, interlined curtains which exactly match the pelmet, wall covering and the corona contribute to a lavish and delightful room.

Cutting the material

See general instructions for cutting on pages 16–17.

Cutting lining and interlining

For the lining and the interlining you will need exactly the same width across the curtain, but they can be cut slightly shorter. This is because the lining and the interlining will eventually be trimmed to end at the top of the final curtain drop.

To determine the cutting length for the lining and the interlining of pencil-pleated curtains, subtract 8cm (3¼in) from the curtain-material cutting length.

Follow the instructions for cutting the curtain material when cutting the lining and interlining, but use the slightly shorter cutting length for each width and omit the pattern-matching.

After cutting, fold up the lining and interlining and set them aside until you are ready to use them.

JOINING THE WIDTHS

Once all of your fabric pieces have been cut, you can machine stitch the widths together. The lining and interlining will need to be joined to make up the same width as the curtain width.

To join widths, see general instructions regarding selvedges, pattern-matching and machine stitching on page 17.

(Remember, whole widths must be placed nearest the centre of the window, and any half-width on the outside.) The diagram on page 68 shows the sample curtain once the widths have been joined and before it has been interlined and lined.

Hemming lining

Each curtain lining must next be hemmed along the bottom edge. Using the short clear plastic ruler to check the measurement as you proceed, fold 3cm (1¼in) of fabric to the wrong side and press along the fold. Then fold the 3cm (1¼in) over again to double the hem, and press again along the new fold. With the wrong side of the lining facing up, machine stitch close to the top edge of the hem and then press to embed the stitches.

INTERLINING THE CURTAIN

The interlining is used to give definite body and depth to the folds of the curtain material, and for this reason it must be securely, but invisibly, linked to the curtain material. This is done with interlocking stitches, which are worked by hand. (See page 18 on joining interlining widths.)

Interlocking the two layers

1 Clamp the interlining on to the table with the top along one end of the table and with one selvedge running lengthwise along the very edge of the table.

2 Gently smooth out the interlining. Then manoeuvre the curtain material (clamping it in place as you position it), right side up, on top of the interlining with its selvedge exactly on top of the interlining selvedge, and the top of the curtain material 8cm (3in) above the interlining, to allow for the turn-down for the pencil-pleat heading. This will mean that the bottom edges of the two pieces will be approximately lined up, the curtain material having been cut 8cm (3in) longer. Do not worry if the bottom edges vary a little.

3 Follow steps 9–13, pages 44–5. The interlocking process is exactly the same.

Turn-backs at sides of curtain

After the interlining has been interlocked to the curtain material, the side edges of the curtain can be turned to the wrong side and stitched in place. The interlining and curtain material are each turned back and stitched separately. Now that the curtain material is interlined you will have to move the curtain gently and with great respect.

Turning back side edges of curtain

1 Turn the interlined curtain right side down on the table, with the interlining facing up and with the top of the curtain at one end of the table and one side edge running along the length of the table edge. Fold 5cm (2in) of the interlining to the wrong side all along the side edge, so that 5cm (2in) of the curtain material extends out past the fold of the interlining. Pin the interlining as you go.

2 Thread a long slim darner needle with thread matching the curtain material and, beginning 30cm (12in) from the top of the curtain material, stitch along the very edge of the pinned and folded interlining. Each stitch must go through to the right side of the material but pick up only a few strands of material each time. Space the small running stitches about 4–5cm (1½–2in) apart. Do not pull the stitches too tight or they will 'pit' the curtain material and pucker the edge of the curtain. Stitch in this way down the whole length of the curtain, ending about 30cm (12in) from the bottom of the curtain and removing the pins as you go. If the stitches went all the way to the top and bottom of the curtain, you would have to cut them away when you come to turning up the hems and turning down the tops.

3 Now go back to the top of the curtain again, and fold the 5cm (2in) of the curtain material which extends past the interlining over the folded, stitched interlining. Gently pull the curtain to the table edge and clamp it along the length of the table, so that you will not need to pin.

4 Using large pyramid stitches, sew the curtain material to the interlining along the edge of the curtain material, again beginning 30cm (12in) from the top. Do not let your stitches go through to the front of the curtain. You will find that working these large stitches is very easy if the curtain is clamped to your right and left as you stitch. Readjust the clamps as necessary, pulling more of the curtain on to the table after you have worked along the whole length of the table. Continue in this way, sewing the curtain material to the interlining and ending

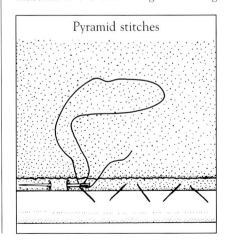

Pyramid stitches

the stitches 30cm (12in) from the bottom of the curtain.

5 After finishing the turn-back on the first side edge of the curtain, unclamp the curtain and pull it with its interlining over the table. As you pull the curtain over, continue to firmly stroke the interlining into place with the palms of your hands, checking that its upper edge remains evenly 8cm (3in) below that of the curtain material (do not worry if this varies a little). Align the other side edge of the curtain with the table edge, then turn back and handstitch as for the first side edge of curtain in steps 1–4.

Curtain hem

The curtain is now ready for hemming. This should never be left until last. You may be tempted to hang your curtains and then hem them, but this is totally wrong. The hemming is part of the process of firmly fixing the interlining to the curtain material. So long as you have very carefully calculated your curtain drop, your curtains will be exactly the right length once they are finished.

Your curtains will hang better if you use lead weights in the hem. You will need only a few weights – one in each corner and one at the base of any seam joining curtain material widths. The type of lead weight that I recommend is a 3cm (1¼in) flat round weight. Other types of weights will not be nearly so satisfactory.

1 Again manoeuvring the curtain with great respect, move the whole curtain so that the hem end runs along the length of the table, keeping the curtain face down. Moving is facilitated by folding the curtain before trying to turn it. Once it is in place it can be unfolded and then left to drop off the far edge of the table. Smooth the fabric out gently and turn up 12cm (4¾in) along the bottom edge of the curtain for the hem, folding the curtain material and the interlining together. Pin horizontally along the edge at the fold, measuring as you go. The edge of the interlining may not be completely even at this stage, but this is irrelevant since it is trimmed back a bit in the next step.

2 Once the entire length of the hem has been pinned, pull back the edge of the curtain material only, leaving the

interlining flat. Evenly trim about 2–4cm (¾–1½in) off the edge of the interlining, so that it measures about 8cm (3in) from the fold in the hem.

3 Once the interlining has been trimmed, smooth the curtain material back over the interlining and turn about 4cm (1½in) *under* the edge of the interlining. Pin this folded edge in place, ending about 25cm (10in) from each side of the curtain to prevent them from being in the way when you are making the corners. Remove the pins that are along the lower edge of the hem close to the corners, but do not sew the hem yet.

4 You are now ready to make the corners of the hem. Move one corner so that it is lined up with the corner of the table. Check that the folded-up hem and the stitched side edge of the curtain meet to form a perfect right

The lovely pale background colour of these curtains, and the height of the pelmet fixed to the ceiling, allow maximum sunlight into the room.

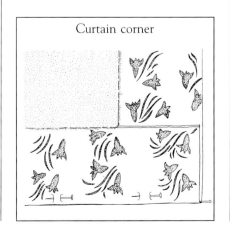

Curtain corner

angle by aligning it with the corner of the table. If necessary, adjust the corner to make it a perfect right angle. After this, slip a closed pair of scissors into the middle of the hem fold (between the two layers of interlining) and pull firmly to smooth out any rucks in the materials. Next, at the exact point of the corner, stick a pin through the curtain material and the interlining.

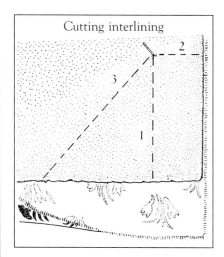

Cutting interlining

5 Then open out the curtain hem and side turn-back until they lie flat on the table with the interlining opened out, carefully keeping the pin in place. You must next trim away the unwanted excess *interlining*. The sharper your scissors are, the more smoothly this operation will go. When trimming, first cut up from the lower edge to the pin, about 5cm (2in) from the edge of the interlining, ending just a *fraction* beyond the pin (**1**). Then cut the interlining from the side edge to the pin to release the 5cm (2in) strip you have just cut (**2**). Lastly cut away the interlining diagonally across the corner (**3**). (The dotted lines in the illustration above indicate the cutting lines just described.)

6 Now the corner can be folded in position. First fold 5cm (2in) of the side edge of the curtain to the wrong side all along the edge, from where the stitching stopped to the very bottom of the curtain (**1**). Then, keeping the side edge folded, fold the curtain material over the diagonal edge of the interlining to form a perfect right angle (**2**). The diagram shows the position of the lead weight within the corner, but do not sew it in yet: see the next step.

Folding the corner

7 Fold the hem up again, turning the raw edge under the interlining at the top of the hem (**3**). Pin along the diagonal of the corner, but do not pin it to the curtain directly below the diagonal. This is because you must now sew the 3cm (1¼in) lead weight in place so that it will not be visible once the corner is folded up. When stitching the lead weight to the corner, be careful not to stitch through to the front of the curtain, but only through the interlining. Also, do not place the lead weight at the very fold of the bottom of the hem, but just above it. Once the lead weight is in place, fold the corner back over it and pin the corner securely in place.

8 Make the second corner in the same way, again sewing a lead weight under the edge of the diagonal at the corner before pinning the corner of the hem securely in place. Then sew a lead weight to the base of any seam in the curtain material where two widths have been joined, unpinning the hem temporarily and placing the weight between the two layers of interlining and just above the fold of the hem. Remove all of the pins along the bottom fold of the hem.

9 Sewing from right to left, slip stitch the hem in place, beginning by stitching up the diagonal at the first corner, then working across the entire hem and ending at the end of the diagonal of the second corner. The stitches must *not* go through to the front of the curtain. Check that the side edges of the curtain are stitched in place all the way to the hem, and complete if necessary. Remove all pins along the hem.

Slip-stitching corner

LINING THE CURTAIN

After the side edges and the hem of the curtain have been stitched in place the lining can be sewn on. It is first stitched to the curtain along one side edge, then interlocked to the curtain and finally stitched to the other side edge of the curtain.

There is no need to stitch the lining to the curtain all the way along its hem, because the lining will be stitched to the hem with every line of interlocking stitches. This is perfectly adequate, especially if you dress the curtains correctly (see pages 78–9).

Sewing lining to curtain
1 Keeping the curtain wrong side facing upwards on the table, manoeuvre the curtain gently in place so that one side edge is running right along the very edge of the length of the table and the lower edge is running along one end of the table. Clamp the curtain to the table in this position. Place the lining right side up on top of the curtain so that the finished hem of the lining (see page 70) is about 3cm (1¼in) from the lower edge of the curtain and so that the side edge of the lining is aligned exactly with the finished side edge of the curtain. Then fold under about 3cm (1¼in) of lining along the side edge of curtain, so that it leaves about 3cm (1¼in) of curtain material exposed between the lining fold and the fold at the side edge of the curtain. The corner of the lining should meet the diagonal fold of the curtain corner. Pin the lining in position as you fold the raw edge under, all along the side edge of the curtain.

Pinning on lining

2 Slip stitch the lining to the curtain along the pinned side edge, stitching only to within 30cm (12in) of the raw edge of the curtain material at the top of the curtain. At the hem of the lining, stitch only about 2cm (¾in) of the lining to the curtain along the lower edge of the lining. Remove the pins as you stitch.

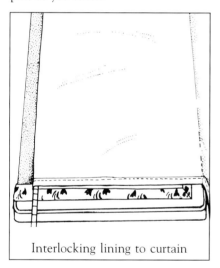

Interlocking lining to curtain

3 You must now interlock the lining to the curtain. Smooth the lining out over the interlining from the edge of the lining just stitched. Measure about 40cm (16in) from this edge of the lining and lay the unfolded 2m (6ft) ruler here, parallel to the curtain edge. Keeping the ruler in this position, fold the lining back over the ruler. Remove the ruler, without disturbing the fold.

4 Interlock the lining to the curtain all along the fold in the same way that the curtain material was interlocked to the interlining (see steps 1 to 3 on page 70), but working the interlocking

stitches about 12cm (4¾in) apart. With each stitch you should prick the needle down through the interlining and back up so that the stitch goes firmly through the interlining, but be careful not to go through the front of the curtain material. Work the stitches to within 20cm (8in) of the edge of the interlining at the top of the curtain; and at the hem of the lining firmly sew the lining to the curtain hem with a few stitches.

5 Work more lines of interlocking stitches across the width of the lining about 40cm (16in) apart in the same way.

6 Once the interlocking is complete, trim the side edge of the lining so that it is even with the edge of the finished curtain. Turn under 3cm (1¼in) of the lining as for the first side edge, and slip stitch it in place.

THE CURTAIN HEADING

The curtain heading is the last part of the curtain to be worked. For the pencil-pleat heading the raw edge of the top of the curtain fabric is folded over to the wrong side and the pencil-pleat tape is machine stitched in place over it.

The heading you make for curtains, pelmets or blinds is an important part of your finished window treatment. You should only ever use the very best heading tapes. In order to ensure that my curtains and pelmets have the most professional headings possible, I only use the best-quality pencil-pleat tape.

Narrow gathering tape
Narrow gathering tape is usually about 2cm (¾in) wide. Because it is not strong enough to bear the weight of heavy interlined curtains, I never use it for curtains. The only time I would use it is for little gathered skirts on dressing tables or for coronas above beds.

8cm (3in) pencil-pleat tape
For most of the curtains I design, which are to go behind a pelmet, I use an 8cm (3in)-wide pencil-pleat tape for the heading. It has three cords which are pulled up to form the narrow pleats. Although this tape is not designed for an exposed curtain heading which is going to be drawn every

day, it is fine for curtains covered by a pelmet. The curtains will hang well with a pencil-pleat heading, so long as they have been properly dressed (see pages 78–9).

The best type of 8cm (3in) pencil-pleat tape is the one with three hook pockets, one above the other. You can move the hooks up or down if any alteration is needed in the length of the curtains. This tape also has the advantage of having each pocket sub-divided so that there is even more room for manoeuvring the hooks to different levels within each pocket. The pockets are placed 2.5cm (1in) apart all along the tape, and when the three cords running along the tape are pulled up the pockets come forward along the right side of the tape and the spaces between the pockets are pushed backwards towards the front of the curtain.

This width of pencil-pleat tape is also perfect for static headings in a pencil-pleated pelmet (see page 82) or an Austrian blind (see page 118).

Other types of heading tape are covered in the section on pelmets (see page 81).

Making the pencil-pleat heading
1 With the curtain still wrong side up on the table and one side edge of the curtain along the length of the table, measure up along the vertical edge of the curtain, from its very bottom to what you have calculated as the *exact finished curtain drop* of your curtains. Then make a pencil mark for the top of the curtain on the lining. Do this at the other side edge of the curtain and at intervals across the width, in order to achieve a straight edge at the top of the curtain.

Then turn the curtain so that the top runs the length of the table. Using the folding ruler and a pencil, draw a line along the lining joining the marks.

2 Taking care not to cut the curtain material, cut the lining and the interlining along the line that you have drawn along the top of the lining. The lining and the interlining now end just at the top (finished) edge of the curtain, and the curtain material will be folded to the wrong side right along this edge.

3 At this stage complete the stitching along the side edges to the top of the trimmed lining. Then trim the curtain material to within 7cm (2¾in) (sufficient for a pencil-pleat heading only) of the newly trimmed edges of the lining and interlining.

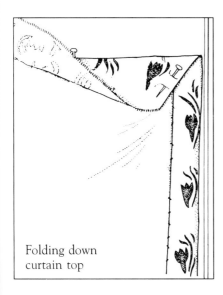

Folding down curtain top

4 Fold the excess 7cm (2¾in) of curtain material to the wrong side of the curtain over the lining, folding the corners in diagonally (see diagram above). Pin the curtain material in place so that the pins are inserted vertically with their heads sticking up beyond the top of the curtain. This is so that they can be removed after the heading tape has been machine stitched to the curtain.

5 There is no need to pin the pencil-pleat tape to the top of the curtain, as you will find it very easy to machine stitch it on without pins. Move your curtain to the machine, taking care not to crease it. At the beginning of the tape pull out the three cords to enable you to turn under about 1.5cm (½in) of the beginning of the tape. Place the *wrong side* of the tape (the hook pockets are on the right side) on the wrong side of the curtain so that it covers the raw edge of the curtain fabric. The folded-under end of the tape should begin as close as possible to the side edge of the curtain without showing at the front. The long edge of the pencil-pleat tape should also be level with the top edge of the curtain. Using a thread which matches, first machine stitch all along the top edge of the tape, close to the edge of the tape, through all thicknesses. When

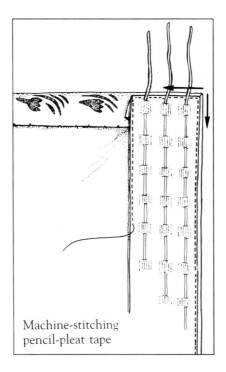

Machine-stitching pencil-pleat tape

you reach within 7cm (2¾in) of the end of the curtain, pull out the three cords, trim the tape and fold the end under as at the beginning. Then complete the stitching by turning a right angle and stitch down the folded-under end of the tape. Go back to the beginning of the tape and machine stitch down the folded end of the tape, then turn a right angle and stitch along the side of the tape, again stitching close to the edge of the tape. The pencil-pleat tape is now machine stitched to the curtain along all four of its sides.

6 The next step is to gather up the heading. This can be quite strenuous work, but here again your wonderful clamps can help. Clamp one end of the heading to the table; this will give you something to pull against. Take hold of the cords in the tape and pull up the curtain to the desired width to cover half the window, the housing space, the return at the outside edge of the curtain and the overlap at the leading edge (see Finished width of pleated curtain on page 66). Pull up from both ends evenly until the desired width is achieved. After you have finished gathering, knot the cords securely together at the leading edge. At the outside edge of the curtain, knot the cords only loosely so

that you can release them to adjust the width if necessary when the curtains are finally hanging in place.

7 Now insert a brass curtain hook in every fourth pocket all along the pulled-up pencil-pleat tape.

FRILLED LEADING EDGE

There are many situations when a frilled leading edge on a pair of curtains looks extremely good: bedrooms, bathrooms, children's rooms, and window treatments with fixed or static heads.

There are important considerations to bear in mind when making such an edging:

– Frilling or pleating must be made out of doubled-over material
– When insetting the frill, it must be piped as well at the seam
– Finished frills should never exceed 4.5cm (2in). Then they will never 'flop' as they attempt to remain horizontal in a vertical situation
– The frilling or pleating must be extremely tight to add to its strength. Permanent pleating is highly recommended (see list of suppliers)
– Always do an inset frill, as opposed to a set-on
– Frilled leading edges are definitely enhanced by the presence of a pair of carefully chosen tie backs, which immediately give the line of frilling a lovely shape

Making a frilled leading edge

1 For a curtain drop of 2.7m (9ft) cut chintz strips 12cm (5in) wide to make a total of approx 6.75m (22½ft) cut on the straight. (We are allowing 2½ times drop.)

2 Join the strips together, and fold longways, wrong sides together with raw edges level. Fold in 1cm at one end to finish off the end. Machine stitch along raw edge with only 0.5cm (¼in) seam allowance. Press.

3 Machine gather (see pages 18–19).

4 Now make up 2.7m (9ft) of piping (see page 21). Stitch on to frilling, raw edges together, with 1.5cm (½in) seam allowance.

5 Now machine stitch piped frill to leading edge, by placing piped side down to right side of curtain material. Stitch on using your zipper foot with

1.5cm (½in) seam allowance. You are bound to find that you have cut off the white selvedge of your material at the leading edge due to the fact it is likely to be at least 2cm (¾in) wide – and would therefore be exposed once you had stitched your frill on.

6 Place the lining on top of frilled curtain, right sides together. Pin across machine stitching on the chintz side.

Now, with zipper foot, stitch along machine line again. Never waver off the line at all since, by doing so, you would risk exposure of the first line of machine stitches, on the front of the piping. Turn and press. Do not trim the seam.

7 Now make curtain in the normal way starting with interlocking the interlining (see step 1, page 70). But

The set-on, contrast-bound frills on the leading edges of these curtains give the curtains and definite and pretty shape, which is accentuated by the tie-backs.

there will be one difference: when you come to turn back the interlining at the leading edge do *not* expose 5cm (2in) of chintz as in step 1, page 70 (bottom). Instead, take interlining right up to your frilled seam and cut it off exactly level with the machine stitches. Now do some long running stitches by hand 1cm (⅜in) away from the machine line. This will totally secure the interlining at the leading edge, which is essential. Now continue making the curtains in the usual way.

SHEER CURTAINS

Lace, voile, muslin or thin silk on the window are beautifully decorative and cast a pretty light on a bedroom. From a practical point of view they are wonderful for privacy.

Making sheers

When you order the material for your sheers, hopefully you can buy exactly the right width for your window size. You must never put more than 1½ times the overall width of the window in the sheer since it would then become too full and therefore far too dense – and would start to darken the room.

When you sew the sheers you must not join any widths together because a vertical seam looks dreadful, and must not have to machine stitch up any raw edges at the sides. These should be selvedges only – and left untouched.

1 For the hem, turn over 3cm (1¼in) and then another 3cm (1¼in). Machine stitch along the very edge of this turning. Press.

Sheer curtains and blinds help to create privacy as well as sometimes screening unsightly views.

2 At the top, arrange a little 2cm (¾in) stand-up heading, and a 2.5cm (1in) channel for the brass drop rod. So press down a 1cm (⅜in) turning at the top and then turn over a further 5cm (2in). Pin and press.

3 Machine stitch along the bottom of this folded edge, just away from the edge, then carefully mark a line 2.5cm (1in) above this machine line. Machine stitch along the line. You have now created the channel for your rod.

Hanging

You need:

- A brass drop rod (1cm (¾in) in diameter) to fit within the recess of your window
- One pair brass ball ends to fit each end of the rod
- Two brass screw eyes (4cm (1½in) long) for stringing up the rod
- One brass cleat, screwed in low down on the architrave to wrap string around
- Several metres (yards) of string – depending on your window height
- Bradawl (spike)

1 With a bradawl make a hole in the timber of the window frame, in the top left and top right corners. Screw in screw eyes so that the eye is facing the adjacent frame, not out into the room.

2 Take one end of the string (let's call it **A**) and feed it up through the right-hand screw eye and then through the left-hand one. Let 20cm (8in) of it hang down on the left while you deal with the other end of the string (let's call it **B**).

Stringing a brass rod

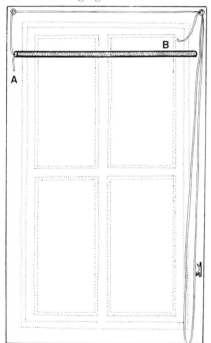

3 Feed **B** through right-hand screw eye and let 20cm (8in) hang down.

4 Screw in brass cleat on right-hand side of window frame somewhere between waist and chest level. This will obviously be hidden behind the curtains.

5 Get the brass drop rod and feed **A** end of string through the hole in the brass ball end. Knot.

6 Feed rod into channel of sheer. Take **B** end of string and feed through hole of other ball end. Knot. Now wrap looped end of string around the cleat when you have pulled the rod up to its highest position.

The advantages of using brass drop rods, as opposed to stretchy wire, to hang sheers are enormous. First, a brass drop rod looks stylish and fits in with the rest of your brass window-furniture accessories. Also the sheer will always hang perfectly parallel to the window sill, whereas stretchy wire over-stretches and sags. Using a cleat, string and screw eyes to lower and raise the sheer (for washing) takes seconds and can be done without having to stand on a stepladder and reach up high.

ATTIC OR VELUX WINDOWS

So often a bedroom, in an attic or loft conversion, ends up with skylight-type windows, totally on the slope of the eave. A particular brand of modern, tilting windows are made by Velux, and are often used to allow maximum light into a bedroom. Curtaining this type of window on an angle, to block out early morning light, can be tricky.

There is a particularly wonderful house in which I have stayed on the west coast of Scotland which has two lovely attic bedrooms. It is a magical place: a nineteenth-century stalking lodge, and one of only two houses on the whole 5000-acre island, which is crawling with red deer and Luing cattle.

In the past, the attic windows were uncurtained. When there was a storm at night you went to bed with the rain and wind lashing against the uncurtained window. You then woke up very early with the dawn glowing in your face – most unsatisfactory, (although very beautiful and inspiring). So, on our last trip there, I insisted that as a house present I would entirely curtain these Velux windows to make the bedrooms much cosier. Here is my method.

The sample curtains

These are the easiest curtains ever to make and hang. They involve virtually no hand sewing; it is all quick machine work. The basic design is a pair of curtains with a stand-up pleat top and bottom, and with narrow gathering tape machined over these pleats to allow brass split rings to be inserted. Brass drop rods are fed through the split rings and then fixed below and above the window. The curtains can be easily drawn well off the window; yet when closed it is still possible to open it for ventilation.

Window size: 92cm long × 80cm wide (3ft × 2ft 8in)

1 For each curtain cut material 1.14m (3ft 9in) long by 1 width.

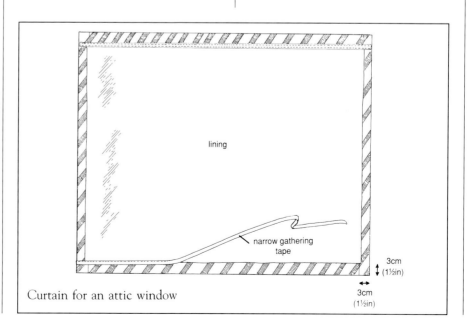

lining

narrow gathering tape

3cm (1½in)

3cm (1½in)

Curtain for an attic window

2 For each curtain cut lining 94cm (3ft 1in) long.

3 With right sides and raw edges together, machine stitch lining to the material at top and bottom, stopping stitches 7cm (2¾in) before each end. Turn.

4 Press the curtain so lining starts and finishes 4cm (1¼in) before the top and bottom. Turn 4cm (1½in) material in up the sides. Then turn in at least 7cm (2¾in) of lining to reveal approximately 3cm (1¼in) of chintz. Hand sew.

5 Machine on narrow gathering tape, to top and bottom of curtain. Each time create a 3cm (1¼in) stand up when you are placing it on. Pull up tape to 50cm (20in) approx. Feed brass split rings into the top every 3cm (1¼in).

6 Screw top brass drop rod into the wall, having already fed on the curtain. You want 5cm (2in) clearance on either side of the window for housing space. The rod must be just above the window. Repeat for lower edge. The great trick is to pull the lower edge tight so the curtain will not sag.

You can easily interline these. Just slip it in at the very beginning and machine stitch it in when you are machining the lining to the chintz. Another attractive feature is to inset a little tightly pleated or gathered frill, made from doubled-over material. The frill should not exceed 3cm (1¼in): preferably a little less. Also, completely plain tie-backs – just like a band or belt 3cm (1¼in) wide – look

Attic-window curtains

good, giving the curtains a lovely shape when open.

HANGING AND DRESSING CURTAINS

Once you have finished your curtains you should try to hang them as soon as possible to prevent creasing. After the curtains are hanging you will need to 'dress' them.

Dressing is the final touch which will give your curtains their highly professional look. Until being made into curtains, curtain material, interlining and lining have only ever been either rolled up on bolts or laid out on tables. After having carefully sewn all three component parts together, it is essential that you now arrange the curtains into regular pleats. Properly dressed, the lining, interlining and curtain material will behave as one body forever after, going backwards and forwards across the window in one fluid movement.

Hanging the curtains

1 Never hang curtains when alone in the house, and preferably not even alone in the room. Accidents can happen. Begin by counting the number of hooks on the curtain to see if they correspond to the number of runners on the rail, including the overlap arm and the screw eyes at the corners of the pelmet board (see page 62). To adjust the number of runners, open the gate at either end of the curtain rail and feed on or remove runners until the number is correct. (This process is clearly described in the manufacturer's instructions.)

2 Climb the ladder with one curtain over your shoulder and begin hooking the curtain to the runners at one end of the pelmet board. Do not begin in the centre of the rail, because the whole weight of the curtain should never hang solely from the overlap arm.

3 Hang the second curtain in the same way as the first.

4 Once both curtains have been hung, check that they overlap at the middle and hug the wall at the ends. If necessary, readjust the pleats by pulling them up or releasing some of the cord until the closed curtains are perfectly gathered. Then at each outside edge of

each curtain, knot the three loosely tied cords together securely. Make sure that no cords are hanging down and showing at the front of the curtain. You can roll these long ends up and sew the roll to the inside of the curtain.

Dressing the curtains

1 Having hung the curtains, cut ten pieces of string, or strips of left-over fabric, each long enough to tie around the curtain when the curtains are drawn open.

2 Open the curtains fully. Then begin pleating the curtains with your hands at about chest level. Stand sideways to the window and close to the right-hand curtain looking towards its outside edge. Place your left hand behind the leading edge of the curtain, so that it points towards the window. (The leading edge *must* point towards the window.) Keeping your hands stretched out and flat so that the fingertips will push out each fold of the pleat, place your right hand behind your left hand, on the right side of the curtain, thus forming the second pleat fold – towards the window. As you form a pleat, first with one hand and then with the other, press the pleated section of the curtain on to your chest to keep the pleats stacked up on top of each other. The depth of the pleats depends on the size of the window. The bigger the window, the deeper the pleats should be. Pleat across the whole curtain in this way. If you end up with the outside edge of the curtain turning towards the room with the lining showing, simply re-pleat the curtains, making the pleats slightly deeper or shallower.

Dressing a curtain

3 Once you have pleated all the way across the curtain, tie a piece of string or a strip of fabric around it. Tie it so that it is tight enough to really hold the pleats firmly but not so tight that it creases the material.

4 Now climb the ladder and repeat the pleating process at the very top of the curtain, matching the pleats to those already made below. Pleat again in three other positions: halfway between the top and the middle, 10cm (4in) from the bottom of the curtain, and lastly between the hem and the middle. Make sure each time to follow *exactly* the size and position of the first pleats you made in step 2. Dress the other curtain in the same way.

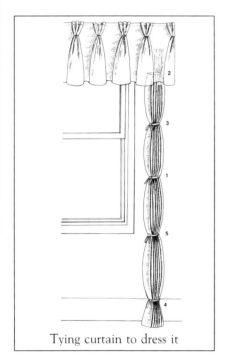

Tying curtain to dress it

5 Having tied up the curtains, I always clap them hard between my hands so that they really get the message! They are very pliable and always respond beautifully. If you can resist closing the curtains, try to leave them tied for at least four days. Then, if treated with respect, they will always hang perfectly in their pleats.

ALTERING LENGTH OF CURTAINS ON SITE

If small problems arise with the length of your curtains once they are already hanging, there are many ways of altering the length without having to touch a stitch.

The reason for the incorrect length of your curtains will not, I am sure, be your measuring ability! It could, rather, be one of the following:

– The builders used a different architrave than planned
– The curtains have come from another house or room
– Your pelmet board cannot be fixed in the planned position because of bad plaster
– You have changed your mind about having so much length in your extra-long curtains (see page 60)

All of these problems are easily solvable and none of the alterations that follow will ever be apparent to the onlooker because they are hidden way up behind the pelmet.

Lengthening by moving hooks
If the hook pockets on your heading tape have subdivisions, one way of lengthening your curtains is to move the hook up to the halfway position in the pocket. This will allow your curtains to gain a little length.

Lengthening with spacers
To gain more length you can put 'spacers' between the curtain rail and the pelmet board. A 'spacer' is a wooden disc about 2cm (¾in) in diameter and 8mm (¼in) thick. It has a hole through the centre, so that a screw can be screwed through it. To lower the curtains, place a spacer between the top-fixing curtain rail and the pelmet board at each screw along the rail. This will, of course, drop the curtain rail only 8mm (¼in), but up to three spacers can be stacked on top of each other between the curtain rail and the board.

If you cannot find these spacers (see the list of suppliers on page 124), it is easy enough to make your own from a piece of hardwood dowelling.

Lengthening with S-hooks
The way to gain even more length for your curtains is to use S-hooks. In this method you will need to take the curtains down (but not the curtain rail, as with the spacers).

S-hooks come in six sizes – 2cm (¾in), 2.5cm (1in), 2.8cm (1⅛in), 3cm (1¼in), 4cm (1½in) and 5cm (2in). First choose the size that will lengthen your curtains to the desired measurement and buy one S-hook for

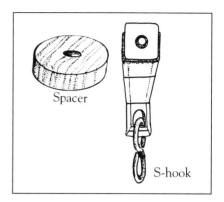

Spacer

S-hook

each curtain hook. Then open one end of each S-hook with pliers so you can slip it on to a runner where the hooks normally go. Once the S-hook is in place, close the end again or it may jump off the runner.

After the S-hooks are all in place, insert the curtain hooks into them.

Shortening by moving hooks
If your curtains are too long, the first option you have available is to move the hooks in the tape to a lower pocket. This will raise the curtains considerably. The pencil-pleat heading will naturally jut forwards, but this does not matter. The fact that the rail is set in the middle of the pelmet board means that the heading can be easily accommodated without ever disturbing the pelmet.

Raising the pelmet board
The spacers used to drop a curtain rail (see above left) can also be used to raise it. In this instance, however, the

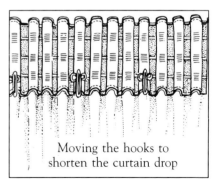

Moving the hooks to shorten the curtain drop

spacers are placed between the horizontal arm of the bracket holding the pelmet board itself. This raises the board and, with it, the curtain rail, thereby raising the curtains.

The pelmet board can also be raised or lowered by attaching it to the wall with slotted adjustable brackets.

9

PELMETS

I am particularly keen on pelmets, as they finish off any window in great style. There are numerous different designs of pelmet that one can use in the bedroom, with either a straight or a curved edge, but the secret of a perfect pelmet is in its proportions. Coronas, half-testers and four-poster beds also use pelmets, and it is best to keep to the same pelmet design for each within a master bedroom.

Choosing a pelmet style

There are many types of pelmet to choose from. Some are suitable for any bedroom, and are explained in this section. Ideas for children's bedrooms are dealt with later (page 116).

Straight edged pelmets:
– Pencil-pleated
– Goblet-pleated
– Smocked-headed
– Velcro-headed with stand-up
– Gathered off a band

Curved edge pelmets:
– Caught-up
– Soft continuous curves
– Arched
– Serpent tail

Whatever pelmet style you choose, be sure to take great care in deciding on the finished drop.

Perfect proportions

I see the pelmet as its 'hat' completing the 'face' of the window. If the hat is too small for the face, it will remind one of a great fat face with a beret that is far too small perched on top. This has the effect of broadening the face all the more. Equally, if the face is long and thin and the hat is similar in proportion (especially if it has deep fringing on its lower edge), then the face will look as if it cannot see out.

There are many different theories on pelmet proportions. I follow the principle that for every 30cm (12in) of drop of curtain allow 5cm (2in) for the drop of the pelmet. This is merely a guide and not a rule, since there are so many variables to consider:

– direction the window is facing
– nature and colour of material
– position of pelmet board
– straight or curved edge of pelmet

To help you, get someone else to hold your 2m (6ft) ruler up against the window with a handkerchief tied around it at the point where you want the bottom of the pelmet. This will help your eye 'lock on' to a particular length, and you can then decide if it is correct, or too long or short.

Finished pleated width of pelmet

The finished pleated width of the pelmet corresponds, of course, to the 'total width' of the pelmet board. When the 'total width' of the board is mentioned in relation to a pelmet, it always includes the returns, since the pelmet must cover the entire edge of the board.

The sample board shown in the illustration below is the size of the board used in many of the pelmet instructions that follow.

Perfect fullness

In general, pelmets should be fuller than curtains. Most of the pelmets that I give instructions for look best with a fullness of about 2 to 2½ times the total pelmet board measurement.

When deciding how many widths of material are needed, multiply the total width of the board by 2½ or 3. Then determine the quantity of your chosen material.

When following the instructions given for the sample pelmets, there is no need to worry about whether the material being used is 120cm (48in) wide or 137cm (54in). This is because the fullness of 2 to 2½ times the total board width is broad enough to cover these small discrepancies.

The three exceptions to this rule for fullness are the smocked-headed pelmet, the soft continuous-curves pelmet and the diamond-buttoned pelmet (see page 89). They all require less fullness. The instructions for each of these styles show how to achieve perfect fullness in each instance.

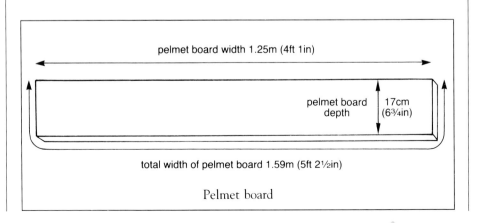

pelmet board width 1.25m (4ft 1in)

pelmet board depth | 17cm (6¾in)

total width of pelmet board 1.59m (5ft 2½in)

Pelmet board

Pencil-pleat tape

This 8cm (3¼in) tape looks wonderful as a pelmet heading when the pelmet drop is no more than 40cm (16in) in length. There is also a deep pencil-pleat tape 14.5cm (5¾in) wide, which I use on deeper pelmets over 40cm (16in), when the narrower tape would look insignificant. You will find that the deeper pelmet is much better balanced by using a deep pencil-pleat tape.

This wider tape has a vertical row of six pockets at equal intervals along it. The rows of pockets are spaced slightly farther apart than three-pocket rows on the 8cm (3¼in)-wide tape.

Smocking tape

Smocking tape is designed for pelmets only. It has a stunning effect especially when, after being pulled up, it is simply hand-smocked with six strands of stranded embroidery floss (see page 86). Again, when buying smocking tape, make an effort to find the best quality available. Inferior smocking tapes will not form the diamond shapes properly when pulled up.

Fusible buckram

If you want a professional finish, avoid tapes that promise to form large pleats for you. They will never have the crispness and elegance of handmade pleats made with fusible buckram, especially if used on a deep interlined curtain or pelmet.

Fusible buckram is a stiff, firm interfacing fabric used to stiffen the headings of pelmets made with goblet pleats (see Glossary on page 123 for an alternative for fusible buckram). It is also used for those pelmets with a piped band about 12cm (5in) wide with gathered 'skirts' coming off them.

The definite, contrast edge on these pencil-pleated pelmets is balanced beautifully by the softer lines of the pink Austrian blinds underneath.

Fusible buckram comes in rolls and is usually available in Britain in three widths – 10cm (4in), 12.5cm (5in) and 15cm (6in). It is wonderful stuff because it tears easily in a straight line, so if you have only a roll of the widest width you can tear it to a narrower width with ease as you unroll it.

When the buckram is used in a heading it *must* be placed between the interlining and the lining and then ironed. The pressing permanently glues it in position. Never make the mistake of placing a hot iron directly on to the buckram because of its heavy glue content. It must always be ironed with the lining covering it completely on the top and with the interlining under it. In this way the glue touches neither the curtain fabric nor the iron.

Cutting length for pelmet widths
As for curtains, the cutting length for each width of pelmet material is determined by adding together the following:

– Finished pelmet drop
– Allowance for hem
– Turn-down at top

The allowances for the hem and the turn-down depend on the type of pelmet you are making, and the measurements are given in the instructions of the individual pelmets.

Pelmet trimmings
Ready-made trimmings or hand-made frills (see page 18) can be added to most types of pelmet, whether it is straight-edged or has a curved edge. When calculating the finished drop of the pelmet, remember to add the length of the trimming.

Calculating material amounts
When calculating how much length to allow for each width of material used in the pelmet, remember to add the length of the pattern repeat (unless you are using a plain material). This means that the drop allowance for each width, as for curtains, is the cutting length plus the pattern repeat.

Don't forget to add the amount needed for any handmade frill or piping when determining how much material you need.

Joining the widths
As for curtains, the widths will have to be pattern-matched when they are joined together (see page 17).

If you are joining an odd number of widths, you can simply join them one after another. However, if your pelmet requires an even number of widths you will not be able to do this because you should never have a seam running up the centre of a pelmet. So, when joining an even number of widths, cut one of the widths in half and place it at either end of the pelmet.

Lining and interlining amounts
Because there is no need for pattern-matching, you will need less lining and interlining than pelmet material. But you must take into account the width from selvedge to selvedge of the lining and interlining. It may not match the width of the pelmet material, and you will have to compensate for this when joining the widths.

I nearly always interline pelmets (with a medium-weight interlining). Not only do they look and hang much better, but the sun will not reveal those endless turnings and bulky seams of inset frills.

Attaching the pelmet to the board
All pelmets are attached to the board with 2cm (¾in)-wide Velcro. The soft side of the Velcro is sewn to the back of the pelmet; and the stiff side is stapled to the front and return edges of the board.

PENCIL-PLEATED PELMET

The pencil-pleated pelmet is one of the simplest to make. It has a soft, informal appearance and is quick and easy to put together.

Perfect proportions
I use a pencil-pleat tape 8cm (3in) wide for pelmets whose drop is between 25cm and 40cm (10in and 16in). On deeper pelmets I would use a 14.5cm (5¾in)-deep tape, since the narrower tape would look too insignificant. Generally I think a deep pencil-pleated pelmet can have a drop of up to about 60cm (24in).

The sample pelmet
The pelmet used as the example in the instructions has a finished drop of 30cm (12in) and a finished width (including returns) of 1.59m (5ft 2½in). The pencil-pleat tape being used is 8cm (3in) wide; however, the techniques used would be the same for a deeper tape.

The cutting length is determined by adding to the finished drop:

– A hem allowance of 5.5cm (2in)
– A turn-down at the top of 5cm (2in)

That makes the cutting length for the sample pelmet 40.5cm (16in).

The cutting length for the lining for this type of pelmet is 2.5cm (1in) less than the finished drop, or 27.5cm (11in) for the sample pelmet. The interlining should be cut the exact length of the finished drop.

The recommended fullness for a pencil-pleated pelmet is about 2½ to 3 times the total width of the board, so three widths are needed for the sample pelmet (assuming the material is 140cm wide).

Cutting and joining the widths
Cut and join the material widths, pattern-matching as you did for your curtains. Cut the lining and the interlining the lengths required, and join them to make the same overall width as the pelmet material. (The lining is not hemmed in the way curtain lining is hemmed.)

Making the pelmet
1 Placing right sides and raw edges together, machine stitch the lower edge of the pelmet material to the lower edge of the lining 1.5cm (½in) from the edge. Stop machine stitches 8cm (3in) before each end. Press to embed the stitches, then press the seam open.

2 Fold the pelmet material wrong sides together along the width of the material 4cm (1½in) below the seam just stitched and press, measuring as you go. This creates a 4cm (1½in) turn-up of pelmet material on the wrong side. The top edge of the lining will now be 5cm (2in) below the top of the pelmet material.

3 With the pelmet lining side up, turn down 5cm (2in) of pelmet material along the top, over the lining; press. The pelmet should now measure 30cm (12in), the finished drop, from top to bottom.

4 Insert the interlining between the pelmet material and the lining so that it fits exactly between the pressed-up hem and the pressed-down turning at the top. Trim 4cm (1½in) off both side edges of the interlining only.

5 Pin the turn-down in place, inserting the pins vertically so that the pinheads stick up above the top edge of the curtain.

6 At the unfinished side edges, fold 4cm (1½in) of the lining and the pelmet material to the inside (between the lining and the interlining), and pin. Slip stitch the lining to the pelmet material to finish the side edges.

7 Machine stitch the tape to the heading and gather the pelmet as for making the pencil-pleat heading for

The fullness of this pencil-pleated pelmet is strongest at its lower edge, giving the line of the pelmet a very definite effect on the window treatment.

curtains (see steps 5 and 6 on page 74).

8 Check again that the finished width of the pelmet is correct. The soft side of the Velcro is now sewn to the back of the pelmet. The top edge of the Velcro should be level with the top edge of the pelmet. Sew the Velcro along the top edge first, bending the heading around your fingers as you sew (see diagram on right) so that the pelmet does not 'shrink' as the Velcro is stitched to it. After sewing the top edge of the Velcro, sew along the bottom edge.

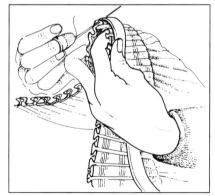

GOBLET-PLEATED PELMETS

Goblet pleats (U.S. 'French pleats') give a lovely, bold effect along the top of your pelmet. Because the pleats are pinched together into three sections only at the base and left open at the top, they look best if they are about 10cm–13cm (4in–5½in) long.

Perfect proportions

It is essential that the depth of the pleats not be too heavy for the drop of the pelmet. The depth of the pleats (and the fusible buckram) should not be more than about one-third of the finished pelmet drop. In terms of maximum drop, these pleats look good on a drop of up to 60cm (24in). The total width of the pelmet (unpleated) should be about 10cm (4in) more than the total length of fusible buckram, due to the insert.

The sample pelmet

The pelmet used as the example in the instructions that follow has a finished drop of 30cm (12in) and a finished width of 1.59m (5ft 2½in). The pleats (and therefore the fusible buckram) are 10cm (4in) deep.

The figure-of-eight knot and swagged cord is a perfect detail to add to a goblet-pleated pelmet.

The cutting length for the material for a goblet-pleated pelmet is determined by adding to the finished drop:

– A hem allowance of 5.5cm (2in)
– A turn-down at the top of 13cm (5in): 10cm (4in) covers the drop of the fusible buckram, and 3cm (1¼in) turns up to hide the raw edge.

This makes the total cutting length 48.5cm (19¼in).

The cutting length for the lining is 26cm (10¼in), and for the interlining is 30cm (11¾in). The recommended fullness for goblet-pleated pelmets is 2½ times the total width of the board, so 3½ widths of 120cm (48in)-wide material are needed for the pelmet.

Making the pelmet

1 Cut and join the widths for the pelmet, pattern-matching every seam.

2 Join 3½ widths of lining. Press seams open. With right sides and raw edges together, machine stitch the main material and lining together along the long side, leaving a gap of 5cm (2in) unstitched at either end. Press the main material to give a hem of 4cm on the wrong side.

3 Join the 3½ widths of interlining together, overlapping seams (see page 18).

4 Insert the interlining between the pelmet material and the lining so that it fits from the fold line of the pressed-up hem to the top of the lining. Trim 4cm (1½in) off both side edges of the interlining only.

5 Keeping the excess pelmet material at the top opened out, fold under 5cm (2in) of the main material, and fold in the lining, to create a 3cm (1¼in) gap between the two folds. Then slip stitch up the side edges of the pelmet.

6 Now unroll some of the fusible buckram, and slip it between the lining and the interlining, either side up. Cut off the amount of buckram you need. The long edge of the buckram should be lined up with the top of the pelmet – i.e. the raw edges of the interlining and the lining – and tucked under the side seam turn-backs at each end, so that it goes up to the very edges. With the lining smoothed out over the buckram, clamp the pelmet heading to the table so that the edges of the buckram, lining and interlining run along the table's long edge. Finish stitching the lining to the material along the side edges to the top of the lining.

7 Press the buckram in place, first making sure that it is completely covered by the interlining on one side and by the lining on the other. You do not want either the material or the iron to come in contact with the glue in the fusible buckram.

8 Having fused the buckram along the full width of the pelmet you can now fold the excess material at the top to the wrong side over the lining. There should be about 13cm (5in) of material extending beyond the top of the lining, but do not worry if this varies a little. Pull the material tightly so as to achieve a very sharp edge. Press.

9 Now turn under about 3cm (1in) along the raw edge of the pelmet material so that the fold is roughly level with the bottom edge of the buckram. Pin this folded-under edge in place, with the pins vertical, their heads downwards. Then at the corners, fold back a diagonal corner as for the corner of a curtain (see step 6 on page 72). Pin this fold in place and press, and only stitch at the diagonal corners. Stitching the rest is unnecessary as the pleats made along the heading will hold the folded top in place. Only the corners are slip stitched in place after pleating.

Calculating for pleats

The diagram below shows the pleat positions and pleat width for the sample pelmet. This is a fairly simple process, but you may find it easier if you draw your pelmet to scale on graph paper as you make your calculations.

Determine how much *excess* there is for the pleats by subtracting the finished width from the flat pelmet width.

Flat, unpleated width:

3.5 × 120cm = 420cm − 12cm (seams)

= 408cm

(3½ × 48in = 168in − 4in (seams)

= 164in)

Excess for pleating:

408cm − 159cm = 249cm

(164in − 62½in = 101½in)

You should allow about 13cm (5¼in) for each pleat, so divide the excess length by 13 (5¼) to find the number of pleats:

249 ÷ 13 = 19 pleats

(101½ ÷ 5¼ = 19 pleats)

Next, calculate the width of the gap between the pleats. The first and last pleat should be placed about 5cm (2in) from the corners of the pelmet board, so place the first pleat, at either end, 22cm (17+5) (8¾in: 6¾+2) from the end of the flat pelmet. (There must never be a pleat on the return of the board.)

With 19 pleats, there will be 18 gaps in between:

159cm − (2 × 22cm) = 115cm

115cm ÷ 18 gaps = 6.38cm

(62½in − (2 × 8¾in) = 45in

45in ÷ 18 gaps = 2.5in)

So, each gap will be 6.38cm (2½in) wide.

Making the goblet pleats

1 With the wrong side of the curtain facing up, mark out each pleat with two vertically inserted pins, one at each side of the pleat. The pinheads should stick up above the top of the pelmet. Move the pins on the wrong side, along the lower edge of the turn-down, to positions in the *gaps* between the pleats. This is essential, otherwise they will either get in the way of the stitching of the pleats or get lost in the pleat once made. The pinheads in the gaps must be pointing *downwards*.

2 Now fold the pleats wrong side together so that the two pinheads marking out the pleat are aligned. Use a sprung clothes peg (U.S. 'clothes-pins') to hold the pleat in place. I tend to peg one at a time, then stitch it.

3 Having pegged the pleat, machine stitch down the side of it. Remove the pins marking the pleat just before stitching. Then line up your short ruler along the line of the side of the pleat, and gently scratch the line into the material along the ruler, ending at the bottom of the buckram, 15cm (6in) from the top of the pelmet. Start stitching about 1cm (¼in) from the top, going backwards over the top of the pelmet, then reverse and stitch forwards down the length of the pleat to the bottom of the buckram. At the end of the buckram again go backwards and forwards to secure the stitching. Cut off excess threads at the

seam ends very close to the stitches. The reason for not starting the stitching at the very top is so that there will be no unsightly ends sticking up above the pelmet. Machine stitch the remaining pleats in the same way.

4 Next lay the pelmet wrong side down and flat on the table with its top edge lying towards you. Hold one pleat along the fold in the middle of the pleat with the finger-tips at the very bottom of the machine stitching. Push the pleat downwards towards the table (and the seam), but only at the lower end of the pleat. The sides bulge outwards, and the pleat now forms into three smaller pleats at the base.

5 Thread a needle with a doubled matching thread. Knot the end of the threads firmly and insert the needle in between two of the three pleats *just* below the buckram, so that the knot will be hidden. Pull the needle out on one side of the triple pleats, halfway between the folded edge of the pleat and the machine stitching, again just below the buckram. Now, to secure the base of the pleat, work three or four stab stitches (vertically worked running stitches) firmly through all the layers of the pleats, working towards the front edge of the pleat. (You have to work the stitches just below the buckram because it is impossible to go through the buckram.) End the stitches 3mm (⅛in) from the edge of the pleat, as the front edges of

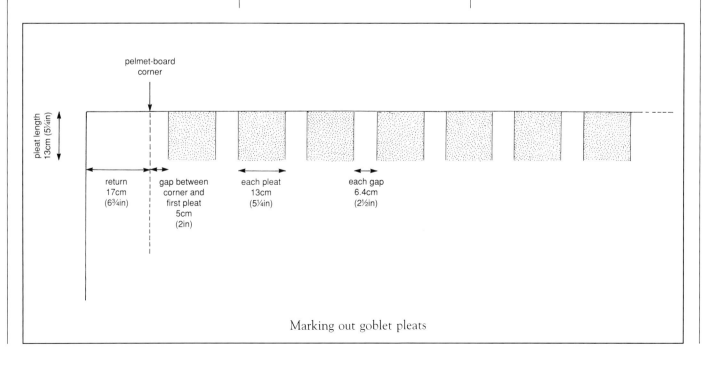

Marking out goblet pleats

the pleat should not be oversewn. The triple folds look much neater with no stitching overlapping them.

6 Pinch each pleat together and hand sew through it at the base as for the first pleat.

7 On the wrong side, slip stitch the corners of the heading fold in place.

8 Stuff each pleat *generously* with scraps of interlining so that it will hold its goblet shape.

9 Sew Velcro to the top of the pelmet as for the pencil-pleated pelmet.

SMOCKED PELMETS

This pelmet heading is just sensational, whichever of the following you choose. The look is so fine, intricate, yet so interesting and ultimately very elegant. The joy is that any of the styles are easy to achieve. You will be happily surprised because although they look as if they take for ever to do, they definitely do not: they are simple.

You must use a long slim, sharp needle with a large eye (for example, a 3/9 Long Darner by Milward). The length of this needle (which I thoroughly recommend for all curtain making) balances well between your fingers; its sharpness allows it to slip through the thickness of the smocking tape without a struggle; the large eye means threading up the silk skein (six strands) is simple. (Never split up the strands – you must use all six.)

It is essential when making a smocked-headed pelmet to use only the best-quality smocking tape. An inferior tape will not pull up properly and the results will not be nearly so good.

The smocking stitches are worked on to the front of the heading after the flat pelmet has been finished and the smocking tape stitched to the back. You can use a matching thread, or a contrast looks very effective.

Perfect proportions and fullness
A smocked-headed pelmet, using the classic smocking tape, can be made with a drop of between 25cm and 45cm (10in and 18in).

For perfect fullness, however, the finished flat width of the pelmet before smocking must be *twice* the total width of the board and *no more*. This is important because otherwise the diamond shapes will not be pulled apart sufficiently.

The sample pelmet
The sample pelmet is the same as for the pencil-pleated pelmet. The smocked-headed pelmet is made exactly as for the pencil-pleated pelmet except that the finished flat width of the pelmet must be exactly 3.18m (10ft 6in) as our sample board is 1.59m, so you will probably need only 3 widths of material, which will then be trimmed at each side after the widths are joined to achieve the correct finished width. When trimming, remember to leave a 7cm (3in) turn-back allowance at each side.

Follow all the steps for making the pencil-pleated pelmet, but, of course, machine stitch an 8.5cm (3¼in)-wide smocking tape to the heading instead of pencil-pleat tape, and do not sew on the Velcro until the smocking is complete. Note that the smocking tape has four cords and must be sewn on with the hook pockets facing upwards or the diamonds will form at the back of the pelmet instead of the front.

Diamond smocking
Thread needed: ½ skein (approx) per material width

1 Once the tape has been gathered up to the correct finished width, you can smock the heading. Don't be discouraged by how untidy and chaotic the heading looks at this stage. 'Pull' each pleat down to organise it in a tidy way.

2 Thread a large needle with six strands of embroidery floss and knot the end. With the right side of the pelmet facing you and working from left to right, pinch the first two pleats at the left together. Pass the needle from back to front, bringing it out 5mm (¼in) to the left of the first pleat fold and 1cm (⅜in) from the top of the pelmet. Then insert the needle from right to left through the first two pleats, 5mm (¼in) to the right side of the second pleat fold and out at the starting point. Then insert it again through the second pleat at the same point it was inserted before but this time pass the needle through the pelmet and out the back. Repeat this process for every pair of pleats across the heading at the same level. The diagrams above show the front and back

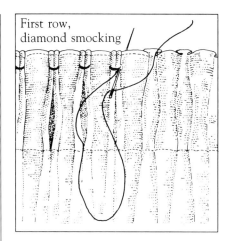

First row, diamond smocking

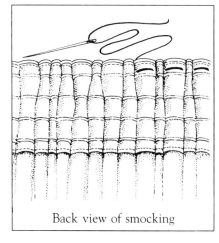

Back view of smocking

of the heading as the first row of stitches are being worked.

3 Now repeat the process, but along the bottom of the tape 1cm (½in) under the machine stitching, sewing the same pairs of pleats together. (By stitching under the machine line it eases the passing of the needle through the pleats.)

4 Repeat the same process along the middle of the tape (see below), but

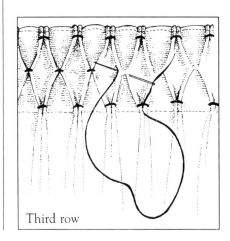

Third row

this time start by sewing the second and third pleats together instead of the first and second, to create the lovely diamond shapes. You do not need to pick up the tape behind while doing these stitches. Just slip the needle through the material pleats.

5 Sew on the Velcro as for the pencil-pleated pelmet.

Outlined diamond smocking

Thread needed: 1¼ skeins (approx) per material width

Repeat all the steps of Diamond Smocking, and then do the following:

1 Thread up your long sharp needle with 50cm (20in) of skein, and knot the end. Don't use any greater length, or it will become tangled. Come in from the back of the pelmet at an existing smocking stitch, and pull the thread all the way through. Now outline the top halves of the diamonds by going under each existing smocking stitch, at the top and then in the centre of each diamond.

diamond instead of the skeins. The effect of this is beautiful, especially on a patterned chintz when you have picked out an appropriate colour which pulls the whole thing together.

In this situation, you may also want to contrast bind the top with a 1cm (½in) binding as an added detail. Obviously the colour of the contrast binding must identically match the colour of the ribbon – which is not always easy to achieve. Buy the ribbon first, then match the contrast to it. With or without the contrast binding the effect is sensational since there is a terrific presence in double-sided satin ribbon.

A wonderful extra detail is to use two different colours of ribbon in the diamond pattern. These must be sewn separately, one after the other.

Diamond smock the entire heading in the usual way. Thread up a large eyed needle with the ribbon, knot the end, and repeat the outlining process in exactly the same way. Pulling the ribbon through from the back to the

front of the pelmet heading is difficult. You just have to be patient and pull the needle hard (wiggling it at the same time) until it eases through. There is a very definite knack to get the ribbon to lie flat in between each stitch. It will automatically twist as you pull it through unless you apply pressure with your thumb as you pull, right by the stitch you are going through.

It is difficult to pull 3m (10ft) of ribbon through with every stitch, so start in the middle of the pelmet, and sew with 1.5m (5ft) at a time. When you come to the end of your ribbon merely knot it at the back or else stitch it down with a few little hand stitches. (It doesn't really matter how many times you finish one piece of ribbon and start another.)

Honeycomb smocking

Thread needed: ¾ skein (approx) per material width

This is a stunning effect and a little more intricate than diamond smocking. The stitching method is the same but you have four rows of stitching not three. You stitch the top (row 1) and bottom (row 4) in the same way as Diamond Smocking. Once you have done that, you need to do the other two rows, rows 2 and 3. Stitch row 2, a third of the way below row 1. Now stitch row 3, a third of the way above row 4.

Outlined honeycomb smocking

Thread needed: 1¼ skeins (approx) per material width

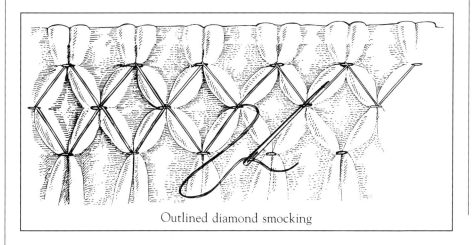

Outlined diamond smocking

2 When you get to the end of the pelmet, go back the other way going along the bottom (and middle) stitches. (It does not really matter whether you now work backwards or else start back at the beginning.)

Outlined diamond smocking with ribbons

Thread needed: ½ skein (approx) embroidery thread; 3m (10ft) ribbon per material width

The theory and method are virtually identical to Outlined Diamond Smocking but you use 3mm (⅒in) double-sided satin ribbons for the

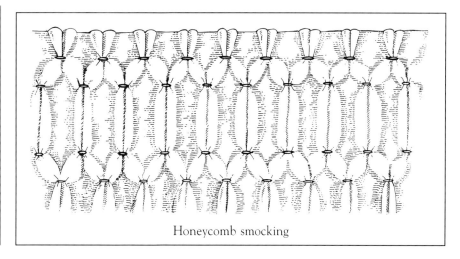

Honeycomb smocking

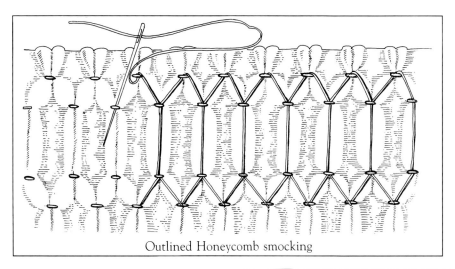

Outlined Honeycomb smocking

Repeat the entire process of stitching as for Honeycomb Smocking. Once you have done that you are ready to outline it. Follow the same procedure as in Outlined Diamond Smocking.

Miniature Diamond Smocking

Thread needed: 1 skein (approx) per material width

This is a wonderful effect on a curtain or pelmet heading. It has the greatest depth and the most intricate character compared with all the previous smocking techniques. Out of all of them, it looks highly time-consuming and expensive but it is really quite simple. There are five rows of stitching in this heading.

Outlined miniature diamond smocking

Thread needed: 2½ skeins (approx) per material width

Repeat the Diamond Smocking process. Then outline it in the same way as Outlined Diamond Smocking. Your diamond shapes are half the size.

Double-depth smocking

Thread needed: 2 skeins per material width

You may have a gathered pelmet that is nearer 45cm (18in) in length, or over, and you want it to have a

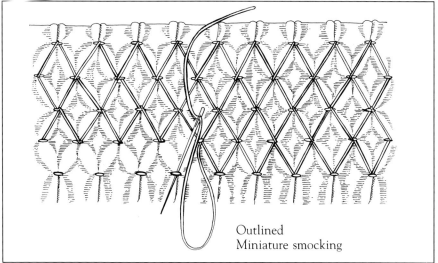

Outlined
Miniature smocking

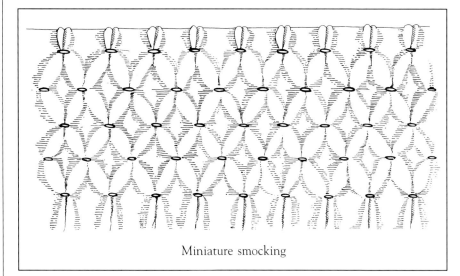

Miniature smocking

1 Smock row 1 and row 5 in an identical way to Diamond Smocking.

2 Now stitch row 3 at the exact centre of the diamond, sewing the same two ridges together as with rows 1 and 5.

3 Now stitch rows 2 and 4 by doing a row in between rows 1 and 3, but stitching the opposite ridges together.

smocked heading. It is essential that your heading is about double the depth of all the previous ones. Those are based on the ordinary 8cm (3in)-deep smocking tape and are highly suitable on pelmets whose drop is between 30–35cm (12–14in). Smocking tape deeper than 8cm (3in) is not obtainable. Stitching together two strips of tape, one on top of the other, to create double the depth is highly inadvisable since it does not really work as the diamonds do not fall in the correct place on the lower row.

The answer to the problem is simple: stitch double-depth pencil pleat on to the top of your pelmet just as if you were doing a double-depth pencil-pleat pelmet. However, instead of stitching the tape merely at its top, bottom, and sides (as you would usually do), you also stitch along the very centre of the tape. By doing this you create an essential guideline for when it comes to the smocking.

1 Stitch on double-depth pencil-pleat tape as just described and pull up to half the width of the total length of the pelmet at its lower edge. Knot very securely.

2 Thread up a long slim needle in usual way. You have five rows of smocking to do. Stitch it on exactly the same way as in Miniature Diamond Smocking. The central machine stitching line now forms a guide for your row 3. The whole thing comes out like the Miniature Smocked pelmet, but double the size.

Outline diamond smocking with buttons

This is a stunning pelmet for any bedroom. I adore it in master bedrooms but it is particularly suitable in a dressing room and in children's (especially boys') rooms. Made out of a strong, masculine material, this design has an extremely orderly and definite character, far removed from frilled, flouncy, curvaceous pelmets.

Thread needed: 1¼ skeins (approx) per material width

Buttons: 57 (approx) × 11mm (½in) buttons (self-covering type) per material width assuming the material is 1.20m (48in) wide – but buy a few more buttons if the material is nearer 1.40m (56in) wide

Contrast material: 20cm (8in) × 1.20m (48in) (approx) of contrast material to cover the buttons

1 Follow all instructions for making a smock-headed pelmet as on page 86.

2 Cover the buttons in the contrast material.

3 Diamond smock the pelmet as on page 87 with a colour matching the contrast buttons. The only difference when you are stitching is that when you come through for the second time on each stitch, sew through the button loop. So you will end up with a button at every point of the diamond.

4 Thread up your long thin needle with your matching smocking thread again, and now outline the diamond smocking, by wrapping the thread once around each button.

White pearl-button smocking

This creates a beautiful effect. Instead of hand covering the metal buttons you can buy extremely pretty pearl buttons in any large haberdashery shop. These look particularly good either on a dark-coloured material (with white in it) or else on a plain chintz. Smock the heading and button it, then outline the diamond shape, in white embroidery thread or else narrow white ribbon (see page 87). Imagine the impact this would have, when on a pale blue, pink, green or yellow chintz in a master bathroom, for example. For children's pelmets you could use, instead, novelty buttons (animals, etc.).

VELCRO-HEADED PELMET WITH A STAND-UP

I love a 'stand-up' along the top of a pelmet. It makes the pelmet look perfectly balanced when it is hanging in place. All pelmets hang down, so why not have a part of them going up as well? This pelmet has a plaited or ruched band sewn over the gathers, and is made without interlining.

Perfect proportions and fullness

The recommended fullness for a Velcro-headed pelmet with a stand-up is about 3 times the total width of the board.

Making the pelmet

Velcro 2cm (¾in) wide is stapled to the edge of the board along the front and along the returns as well. The excess at the top of the pelmet is determined by how long you want the stand-up above the board to be. I would probably use a stand-up of about 4.5cm (1¾in).

1 Follow all the steps for making the pencil-pleated pelmet, remembering to add an extra for the stand-up at the top.

2 With the lined and finished flat pelmet wrong side up on the table, measure 4cm (1½in) down from the top edge of the pelmet and make a pencil line on the lining. This is the position of the underside of the board.

3 Cut the Velcro to exactly fit the board. Staple the hard side on to the board.

4 Take the soft side of the Velcro, measure along it, and make a pen mark every 10cm (4in). Number each mark. Then measure along the line on the pelmet lining, marking every 30cm (12in) with a number.

5 As you gather or pleat the pelmet, match up the numbers on the Velcro and the lining. Then, if you are taking up too much or too little, you can adjust the gathering as you go along.

When you have finished the top line go back to the beginning, and stitch along its lower edge. Stitching this lower edge is easier, since you simply pull the pelmet perpendicular to the Velcro as you machine stitch and the pleats (or gathers) form automatically.

6 Make a ruched or plaited band (see Tie-backs on page 98) and hand sew it to the front over the parallel lines of stitching. The band should be wide enough to cover the machine stitching on the front of the pelmet.

7 To hang the pelmet, simply attach the heading to the stiff Velcro previously stapled along the front of the pelmet board and the returns.

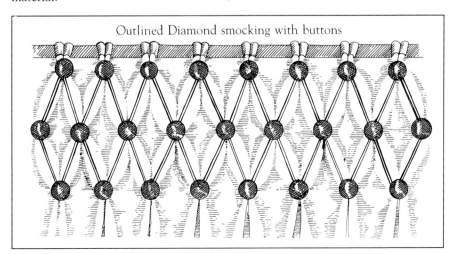

Outlined Diamond smocking with buttons

GATHERED PELMET WITH BAND

The gathered pelmet with a fusible-buckram band has a lovely old-fashioned look about it. This type of pelmet would traditionally have been found hanging from the canopies and bases of imposing four-poster beds.

A gathered pelmet with band must be hung from a pelmet board with a plywood fascia (page 62).

Perfect proportions

The depth of the band should be about one-third of the finished drop of the pelmet, so that the remaining two-thirds consist of the skirt. The longest you could make this pelmet would be 50cm (20in), allowing for a buckram band of 15cm (6in) and a skirt of 35cm (14in).

Perfect fullness

The fusible-buckram band on this pelmet is, of course, the exact measurement of the total pelmet-board width,

ABOVE *The pelmets on the window and the four-poster echo each other in every detail. The window pelmet is correctly shallow due to the minimal clearance caused by the ceiling beam.*

ABOVE, RIGHT *A peaceful style of pelmet with a contrast-bound gathered skirt off a contrast-piped fusible buckram band. The same details are echoed in the window treatment.*

but the gathered skirt should be about 2½ to 3 times this measurement. To ensure a light appearance, the skirt is usually not interlined, although the buckram band is. (If interlining is required for the gathered skirt, only a lightweight interlining, or domette, should be used.)

The sample pelmet

The sample pelmet has a finished drop of 30cm (12in) and a total finished width of 1.59m (5ft 2½in). The buckram-stiffened band is 10cm (4in) deep, and the skirt has a 20cm (8in) finished drop.

The cutting length for the skirt material is determined by adding to the finished drop of the skirt:

– A hem allowance of 5.5cm (2in)
– A seam allowance at the top of 1.5cm (½in)

This makes the cutting length for the sample skirt 27cm (10½in). The lining for the skirt has a cutting length 1cm (½in) shorter than the finished drop, which gives 19cm (7½in) for the sample pelmet. The sample pelmet skirt requires four widths of material.

The band piece has a seam allowance, top and bottom, of 1.5cm (½in); and should have a turn-back allowance at each end of 4cm (1½in). So for a 10cm (4in) band you will need to cut the band material 13cm (5in) deep and 1.67m (5ft 5½in) long. The lining should be cut exactly the same size as the band material. The interlining for the band should be cut to the width of the finished band – in this case 10cm (4in) – and the same length as the band material and lining.

Cutting and joining the widths

Cut and join the widths as explained for the pencil-pleated pelmet.

Covering the piping cord

Both the top and bottom of the band are edged with piping cord. The cord is best covered in a contrasting colour. Cut two pieces of piping cord, each the total length of the pelmet board, and cover the cords (see page 21).

Making the pelmet

1 Placing right sides and raw edges together, machine stitch the covered piping cord to the top of the band

material 1.5cm (½in) from the edge (close to the cord), first positioning the cord so that it begins and ends 5cm (2in) from each side edge. Sew the other cord to the bottom of the band in the same way.

2 Placing right sides and raw edges together, machine stitch the band lining and material together along the top 1.5cm (½in) from the edge.

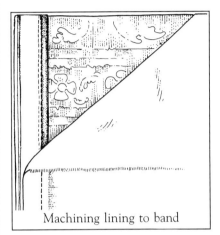

Machining lining to band

3 Cut a piece of soft 2cm (¾in)-wide Velcro the exact total width of the pelmet board. Now machine stitch the Velcro to the very top of the right side of the lining only, as close to the piped cord as possible and all around the Velcro (see below). The Velcro is 5cm (2in) shorter than the lining at each end to allow for turn-backs.

4 With the right sides and the raw edges together, machine stitch the lower edge of the skirt material to the lower edge of the lining 1.5cm (½in) from the edge. Stop stitches 7cm (2¾in) before each end. Press the seam open. Fold the lining and the skirt material wrong sides together, so that the top raw edges are level, and press the hemline fold. Turn in 5cm (2in) at the side edges and slip stitch the lining to the skirt material. Press. Machine stitch along the top edge of the skirt 1.5cm (½in) from the raw edge through both skirt and lining. Then machine gather the skirt to fit the total width of the pelmet board (see page 18 for machine gathering).

5 Now, placing right sides and raw edges together, machine stitch the finished skirt to the lower edge of the band material 1.5cm (½in) from the edge. Trim the seam. Then fold 4cm (1½in) approx to the wrong side along the band material and lining at the side edges; press.

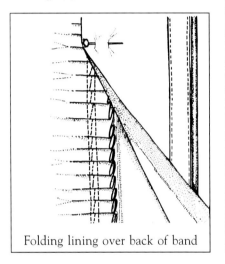

Folding lining over back of band

6 Insert a strip of interlining exactly the finished size of the band. Then insert a strip of fusible buckram exactly the same size as the interlining and place on top of it. Pull the lining tightly over the back of the band to cover the buckram, turn under the lower edge just below the raw edge of the gathered skirt; pin. Slip stitch the lining in place. Press the back of the band so that the heat will glue in the fusible buckram in place.

CAUGHT-UP PELMET

The caught-up pelmet is a sensational one – soft and natural and not at all regimented. It is extraordinarily easy to put together, but has the satisfying quality of appearing highly complicated and difficult to achieve. It is the perfect way to achieve a stunning window treatment when you want soft curves which look less tailored than swags and tails.

Perfect proportions and fullness

This pelmet is made in exactly the same way as the gathered pelmet with a band, and the same rule for fullness applies.

The proportions, however, are slightly different because the skirt is caught up; therefore the band should not be as deep as one-third of the total drop. This pelmet will not look good on a window whose drop is under 2.40m (8ft) or whose width is under 1.25m (4ft 1in).

The sample pelmet

The sample pelmet has curtains with a drop of 2.60m (8ft 7in) and a total pelmet-board width of 1.71m (5ft 7½in). The buckram band is 12cm (4¾in) deep and the skirt is 60cm (2ft) long.

The pelmet is made in exactly the same way as the gathered pelmet with a band. Then once the pelmet is hanging in place it is caught up at intervals as explained below.

Catching up the pelmet

1 Find the centre of the pelmet, and mark it with a pin on the lower piping line. This is point **B** on the diagram below. Then mark points **A** and **C**, equidistant from **B** as shown. These are the positions where the pelmet will be caught up.

2 Mark points **E** and **D** below point **A**. Pinch the material together at **D** and raise it up to point **E**, then pinch together the material at **E** and raise points **D** and **E** together to point **A**; pin. Using a strong matching thread, sew the folds in position with about four small stitches.

3 Catch up the skirt in the same way to points **B** and **C**.

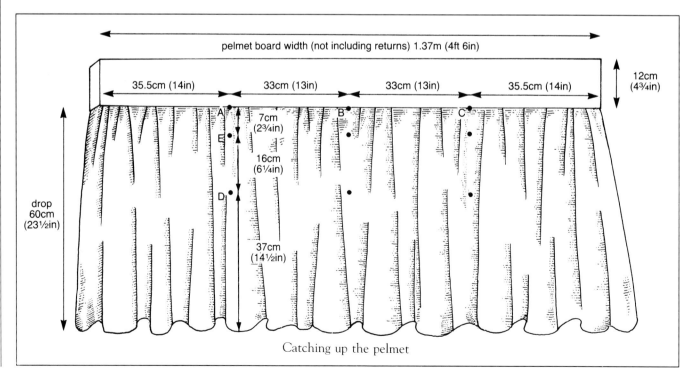

Catching up the pelmet

4 Make three flower rosettes (see page 103) and sew one on top of each set of tucks.

SOFT CONTINUOUS-CURVES PELMET

The soft continuous-curves pelmet is especially beautiful in a bay window. The joy of it is that it works so well with so many different proportions and details, so you can make it as simple or elaborate as you like.

You must always interline this pelmet. It is also essential that it have a trimming of some description along the lower edge. The trimming is needed to accentuate the lovely shape and rhythm of the continuous curves.

Perfect proportions

The shorter version of this pelmet should never have a finished drop of less than 20cm (8in) at the shortest point. The longest version I tend to

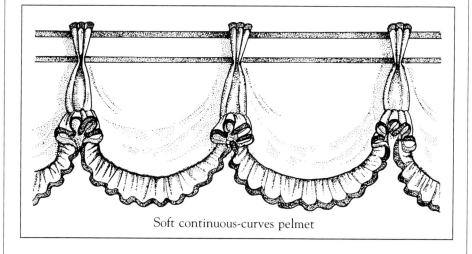

Soft continuous-curves pelmet

make has a drop of 40cm (16in) at the shortest point. The longest point on the pelmet should be about 10cm (4in) more than the shortest in order to give it an attractive curve.

Perfect fullness

The perfect fullness for this pelmet is a finished flat width of 1½ times the total pelmet-board width, which makes it a very economical pelmet in terms of material. One goblet pleat is placed above the centre of the shallowest part of each curve to take up the excess material.

The sample pelmet

The sample pelmet is intended for curtains that have a drop of 2.70m (8ft 10½in). The total pelmet-board width is 2.20m (7ft 3in). The finished drop of the pelmet at the shortest point is 30cm (12in) and at the longest point, 40cm (16in). The pelmet has a hand-made inset frill (see page 18).

The finished flat (or unpleated) width of the sample pelmet is 3.30m (11ft).

The pelmet material, lining and interlining are cut with the aid of a template. The top of the sample pelmet is interfaced with a fusible-buckram band 10cm (4in) deep.

Making the template

1 You can make your template out of newspaper (see page 48). Once you have determined the finished drop at the shortest and the longest points, you must decide how wide to make each curve. The sample pelmet has a curve 55cm (21½in) wide, so draw two vertical parallel lines this far apart.

2 Now draw a horizontal line across the top. For a buckram band 10cm (4in) wide you need a turn-down of 13cm (5in) at the top (see *Goblet pleats*, page 84). Draw a horizontal line this distance below the first line to mark the position of the finished top of the pelmet.

3 Now mark the point of the longest drop at both sides of the template and the shortest drop at the centre of the template. Use a piece of piping cord as a guide in drawing the curve between these points. Then add a 1.5cm (½in)

seam allowance along the bottom of the curve. Cut out the template.

Making the pelmet

1 The cutting length for the pelmet material is 54.5cm (21½in). Cut and pattern-join enough widths to make up a width of 3.40m (11ft 2in). This is 10cm (4in) more than the finished flat width of the pelmet to allow for a 5cm (2in) turn-back at each side edge.

2 The cutting length for the lining and the interlining is 13cm (5in) less than the pelmet material, or in this case 41.5cm (16¼in). Cut and join the lining and interlining to make up the same width as the pelmet material.

3 Use the template to mark the shape on to the pelmet material. Fold the material in half vertically, right sides together. Place the edge of the template on the centre fold; pin. Draw along the template curves. Then move the template along and repeat the process. Do this to the end of the material. Keeping the pelmet material folded in half, cut along the marked curved line.

4 Use the cut pelmet, opened out, as the template for the lining and the interlining.

5 Make the inset frill (see page 18) long enough to fit along the lower edge of the pelmet, and machine stitch it to the lower edge of the pelmet material as instructed in the inset-frill instructions.

6 Place the lining on the pelmet material with right sides facing, and pin them together very carefully along the lower edge. Place the interlining on top of the lining and pin along the same edge.

7 With the wrong side of the pelmet material facing upwards, machine stitch the layers together just inside the stitching used to attach the frill to the pelmet.

8 Trim the interlining close to the seam. Then trim the pelmet material, frill and lining seams to 5mm (¼in), and clip the seam allowance at intervals to ease the curve. Turn the pelmet right side out and press on the wrong side.

9 Trim 5cm (2in) off the interlining at each end. Then fold 5cm (2in) of the pelmet material and the lining to the

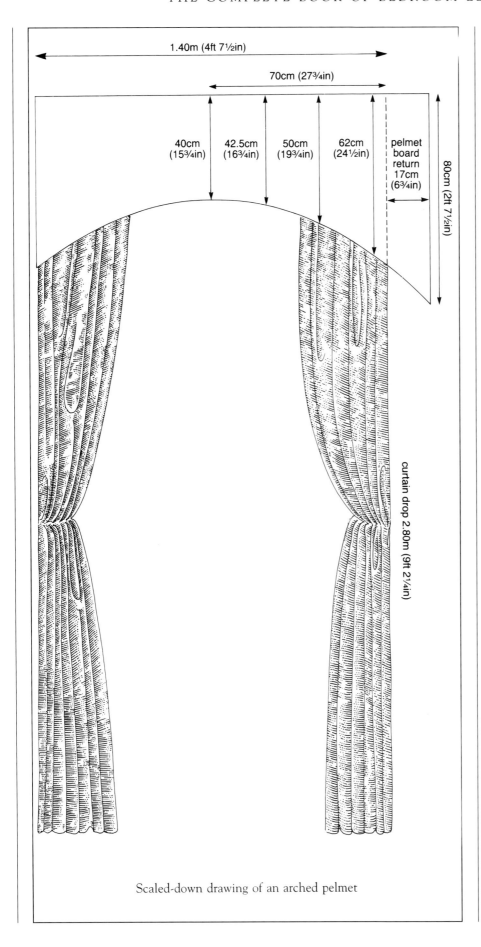

1.40m (4ft 7½in)

70cm (27¾in)

40cm (15¾in)

42.5cm (16¾in)

50cm (19¾in)

62cm (24½in)

pelmet board return 17cm (6¾in)

80cm (2ft 7½in)

curtain drop 2.80m (9ft 2¼in)

Scaled-down drawing of an arched pelmet

inside and slip stitch the lining to the pelmet material.

10 Follow steps 5–7 of making the goblet-pleated pelmet, but making only one goblet pleat centred above shortest part of each curve. To work out how large each goblet pleat should be do a very simple calculation. Subtract the finished size of the pelmet from the flat, unpleated size. Then divide this sumby the number of 'up' arches in the pelmet.

ARCHED PELMET

This pelmet exudes elegance if correctly cut and proportioned. It requires no template; the single continuous curve is merely marked out with a series of dots or pins and then cut. The secret is to be bold when cutting and to understand the proportions of the pelmet in relation to the drop and width of the window.

It is essential to trim the lower edge of this pelmet with some sort of contrast, whether fringe or a handmade gathered frill. Without a trimming the pelmet loses much of its impact.

This pelmet is fairly extravagant on material since there is a lot of wastage in the central sections when cutting. However, it is likely that you will be using this wastage to make your frill or perhaps to make a tie-back, so do not worry.

Perfect fullness
An arched curve will hang beautifully, provided it is fairly full. Therefore you should allow about 3 times the total width of the pelmet board if you are making a pencil-pleat or goblet-pleat heading. You can use other headings, but make sure that you use the correct fullness for whichever heading you choose.

Perfect proportions
By far the best way to work out the proportions is to make a scale drawing on graph paper. Draw the whole window to scale with the curtains in place. Then, on a separate sheet, draw the pelmet to scale and cut it out. Then place it on top of the curtained window drawing to test the size (see the illustration left).

On a fairly tall and narrow window, for example 2.90m by 1.40m (9ft 6in

Although the window pelmets are arched, and the half-tester pelmet is straight, there is a definite sense of harmony in this room. Note that the half-tester has a stand-up to balance the moulding above the window.

by 4ft 7in), you should nearly always cut the pelmet so that the central drop is half the side drop at the end of the return. On a much wider window you will need to ease the sharpness of the curve.

The sample pelmet

The sample pelmet is shown in the diagram on page 94. It has a finished centre drop of 40cm (16in) and a side drop of 80cm (2ft 7½in). The total width of the pelmet board is 1.74m (5ft 9in). It requires four widths of material. There is an inset frill along the lower edge, and it has a 14.5cm (5¾in)-deep pencil-pleat heading.

The cutting length for the pelmet material is determined by adding to the finished side drop:

– A seam allowance at the lower edge of 1.5cm (½in)
– A turn-down allowance at the top of 10cm (4in)

This makes the cutting length for the sample pelmet 91.5cm (3ft).

The lining and interlining are cut 10cm (4in) shorter, since they have no turn-down allowance. But note that when joining up the lining, you must use pelmet material for the last 40cm (16in) at both side edges. This is so that the lining will not show at the lower edge of the returns.

Cutting and joining the widths

1 Cut and join the widths.

2 Now fold the pelmet material in half, right sides together. Measure and mark the positions of the central drop, the drop at the side and three places equally spaced between (see page 94), taking the turn-down and the bottom seam allowance into account. Now lay a piping cord along these points to join them into a gradual curve. Ease the sharpness of the curve

95

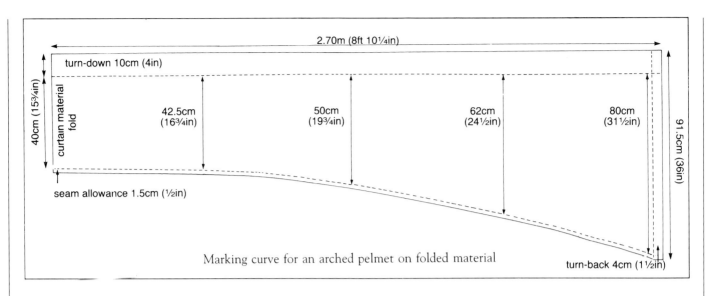

2.70m (8ft 10¼in)

turn-down 10cm (4in)

40cm (15¾in)

curtain material
fold

42.5cm
(16¾in)

50cm
(19¾in)

62cm
(24½in)

80cm
(31½in)

91.5cm (36in)

seam allowance 1.5cm (½in)

Marking curve for an arched pelmet on folded material

turn-back 4cm (1½in)

as it approaches the centre so that you do not end up with anything remotely resembling a V-shape at the centre – it should really be fairly flat at this point.

3 Having decided the shape, draw a line along the piping cord and cut. Your scissors must be absolutely parallel with the top when you reach the centre and not pointing upwards.

4 Open out the pelmet material and use it as a template for the lining and interlining.

Making the pelmet
The pelmet is made up exactly as for the soft continuous-curves pelmet, except that the heading is made as for the pencil-pleated pelmet.

SERPENT-TAIL PELMET

The serpent-tail pelmet has such an attractive gently rhythmic shape. It looks equally good if the tail is cut either very long (half the overall drop of the curtains) or fairly short. The trick, as with the arched pelmet, is to cut the shape with great confidence. Again, it is an absolute necessity to have a trimming along the lower edge to accentuate the curve.

Perfect proportions and fullness
The fullness is the same as for the arched curve pelmet. Bear in mind, when deciding on proportions, that LENGTH IS ELEGANCE where all window treatments are concerned, and this pelmet is no different. Decide on the finished drop for the centre, being generous on length since you are going to gain light from the two shorter parts of the pelmet. There must be a marked difference of at least 15cm (6in) between the drop in the centre and the drop at the two highest points (see right).

Decide the shape of the pelmet and make it in the same way as for the arched pelmet.

This room exudes terrific elegance due to the perfectly arched pelmets on each of the four windows. Their shape is beautifully picked out by the contrast-bound frill on the lower edge.

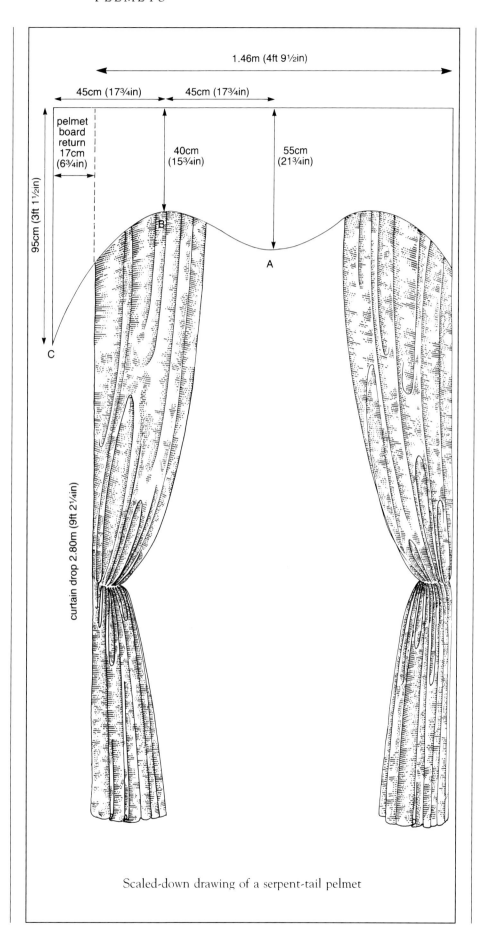

Scaled-down drawing of a serpent-tail pelmet

10

TIE-BACKS, ROSETTES AND BOWS

These details may be small, but they play a significant part in the overall effect of your bedroom. Lovely effects can be achieved by using the same elements in different parts of the room, such as caterpillar in tie-backs and a pelmet, or similar rosettes on a dressing table and on a half tester.

TIE-BACKS FOR BEDROOMS

I am not greatly in favour of tie-backs. Often, they are most suitable when the curtains are cut a little bit too long on purpose. Then a tie-back is seriously necessary to control the curtain when it is drawn back and to give it a lovely shape. Since I rarely ever finish a curtain anything over 1cm (⅜in) too long, I am usually happier to have no tie-back on a bedroom window. (There are not many men who care for tie-backs, and they certainly do not like to hook them round in the morning.) However, having said this, tie-backs are another excuse to be delightfully decorative in yet another detail in your bedroom soft furnishings.

In a bedroom, details such as these are allowed to be very feminine and pretty if you want them to be. The bow or knot type of tie-back looks stunning in bedrooms.

Brass roses look marvellous with corona curtains but I feel rope and tassels for tie-backs are a little grand, formal and severe for a pretty bedroom. They are far more suited for living and dining rooms.

Reasons for tie-backs
– When the curtains are deliberately cut too long they can look disorganised and untidy when drawn back, unless they have a pair of tie-backs to hold them in place

– When maximum light is essential: to hold the curtains off the window, as far as possible
– When it is necessary to try and take the height of the ceiling up a bit, as an optical illusion. Placing the pelmet board as high as possible, then placing tie-backs as low as possible (probably level with your window sill), should give you the optical illusion of the windows being taller than they actually are
– To give the window treatment added shape. Making the curtains curve in and out again adds to the general elegant effect

Size of the tie-back
It is imperative that you do not attempt to make any tie-backs until after your curtains are hanging. Things look so different when the window is finally dressed. You may even decide you don't want a tie-back at all. But, once hanging, you can judge exactly how much these curtains should be held off the window, or exactly how loose it is necessary for the curtains to be.

Get a tape measure and ask someone to hold it around the curtain while you stand back and evaluate the situation. Thus you can decide on the perfect length, style, and thickness to suit your window treatment. Now screw your brass loop-hook in place and make your tie-back.

PLAITED TIE-BACKS

These look particularly suitable in bedrooms, especially if the pelmet of the window or corona involves a plaited band as well. They are very fashionable and look particularly good if one of the three strips of the plait is done in a solid colour, contrasting with the printed chintz.

The sample plaited tie-back
The tie-back used as the example in the instructions has a finished length of 60cm (23½in) and is 5cm (2in) wide after plaiting. Note that when you plait the stuffed tubes, you will lose 25 per cent of the original length. So be sure to add this amount to the desired finished length when deciding on the length of the strips for the tubes. It is probably best to add a little more than this just to be safe. You can then trim the tie-back before finishing off the end.

If you want a thinner or thicker plait than the sample one, just make the tubes narrower or wider as desired. What is essential is that the interlining stuffing should always be cut

Pretty, bow tie-backs are used here to hold the corona curtains back, and to add an extra, feminine detail to a soft and restful room.

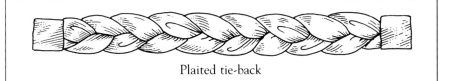

Plaited tie-back

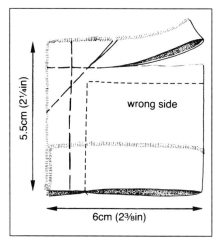

5.5cm (2¼in)

wrong side

6cm (2⅜in)

approximately 50 per cent wider than the tube material.

Materials for plaited tie-backs

For making plaited tie-backs the only materials required are as follows:

– Remnant of curtain material
– Medium-weight interlining
– Matching thread
– Four rings 1.5cm (½in) in diameter

If you do not have enough curtain material left over, then determine the exact dimensions of the tube strips before purchasing any extra material.

Making plaited tie-backs

1 Cut three strips of material, each 9cm by 80cm (3½in by 2ft 7½in). (As suggested it is advisable to cut one of the strips in a contrasting colour.)

2 Fold one strip in half lengthways, with right sides together. Machine stitch along the long side 1.5cm (½in) from the edge and across one short end. Do not press. Trim the seam to 8mm (¼in). Seam the remaining strips in the same way.

3 Using large scissors to push from the short seamed end, turn each tube right side out. Cut off the seam at the short end of each tube; its only purpose was to assist in turning the tubes right side out. Now it is removed so that the seam can be positioned up the centre of the back of the tube. *Never press the tie-back tubes* (except for tie-backs with 'ears').

4 Cut three strips of medium-weight interlining 13cm by 80cm (5in by 2ft 7½in).

5 Cut a piece of string 10cm (4in) longer than the tube, and tie it firmly to the neck of a slim teaspoon. Tie the other end of the string to one of the strips of interlining. Drop the spoon, handle first, down the tube. When the spoon appears at the other end of the tube, pull it to draw the interlining into the tube. The beginning of the interlining, where it is tied to the string, may need to be pinched to-

gether slightly before it will start to go down the tube, but once the end is in it will pull through smoothly. Pull the interlining through until the untied end of the interlining is level with the end of the tube. Now untie the string. Stuff the remaining tubes in exactly the same way.

6 Pull back 2cm (¾in) of material at one end of each tube, and trim 2cm (¾in) off the end of the interlining. It is necessary to remove this bulk so that the three tubes can now be sewn together at this end. Lay the tubes right side up, one on top of the other and with the seams at the centre of the back, and machine stitch them together 1.5cm (½in) from the end.

7 Clamp the machine-stitched end to the edge of the table and plait the three tubes together; pin the ends together. Now check that the tie-back is the desired length, measuring from one raw edge to the other (the ends will not be folded back but bound with another piece of material). Unpin the ends and trim them if necessary. Then trim 2cm (¾in) off the end of the interlining inside each tube and stitch the ends together in the same way as at the beginning of the plait.

8 Now bind the ends of the tie-back. Using material that matches two of the tubes, cut a piece measuring 12cm by 7cm (4¾in by 2¾in). Turn under 1.5cm (½in) along one longer side; press. Then fold the material in half widthwise, right sides together, and machine stitch along two sides, 1.5cm (½in) from the edge, leaving the edge with the turn-back open. Trim the seam to 8mm (¼in), and clip off the corner close to the stitching. Turn binding right side out and slip it on to

one end of the tie-back. Hand sew it firmly in place. Bind the other end in the same way.

9 Sew a ring to the back of the end of the tie-back just bound, so that it extends halfway past the edge. Bind the other end of the tie-back in the same way, and sew on another ring. Make the second tie-back in the same way.

TWISTED TIE-BACKS

The twisted tie-back is very similar to a plaited tie-back, but only two tubes are used instead of three. The twists are held together by being stitched to a stiff band. The twisted tie-back looks best when one of the tubes is in a contrasting colour.

The sample twisted tie-back

The tie-back used as the example in the following instructions has the same finished length as the sample plaited tie-back and is about 3cm (1¼in) wide when finished. The length of the strips for making the two tubes is determined in the same way as for the plaited tie-back (above).

Materials for twisted tie-backs

The materials for the twisted tie-backs are the same as for the plaited tie-backs, with the addition of fusible buckram for the backing band. The

Twisted tie-back

buckram used is the same as the buckram used for hand-pleated headings.

Making twisted tie-backs

1 Follow steps 1–6 for making the plaited tie-backs (page 100), but make only two tubes instead of three.

2 Now make the buckram-interfaced backing for the tie-back. Cut a strip of buckram 60cm by 2.5cm (23½in by 1in). Cut a piece of material to match one of the tubes, measuring 63cm by 8cm (24½in by 3in). Machine stitch this strip and turn it right side out as for the other tubes. Slip the buckram into the tube, positioning the seam at the centre back. Fold the raw edges of the material to the inside at both ends and sew the ends together by hand.

3 Clamp the machine-stitched end of the tubes on to the edge of the table. Wrap the two tubes around each other and pin them together at the end. Now check that the tie-back is the desired length, measuring it 1.5cm (½in) from the raw edge at one end to 1.5cm (½in) from the raw edge at the other end (this allows for the turnbacks). Unpin and trim one end if this is necessary. Then trim 2cm (¾in) off the end of the interlining inside each tube and machine stitch the ends together in the same way they were stitched together at the beginning of the twist (see step 6 on page 100).

4 Folding the seam to the wrong side (between the twists and the band) at each end, hand sew the twisted tie-back to the buckram-interfaced band.

5 Sew a ring to the back of each end of the tie-back so that they extend halfway past the edge. Make the second tie-back in the same way as the first.

CATERPILLAR TIE-BACKS

Caterpillar, or 'ruched', tie-backs are gorgeous. They perfectly complement the ruched headings of curtains slotted on to poles, as well as curtains or pelmets with a stand-up heading

that has a ruched-band detail (see page 21).

Instructions are given for making three types of caterpillar tie-backs: simple caterpillar tie-backs, caterpillar tie-backs with 'ears' and caterpillar tie-backs with contrasting 'ears'. A caterpillar tie-back with 'ears' is a ruched tie-back which has a frill along both sides. All three types of caterpillar tie-back are very easy to make.

The sample caterpillar tie-back

The simple caterpillar tie-back used as the example in the instructions has a finished length of 60cm (23½in) and a finished circumference of 9cm (3¾in). Both of the sample caterpillar tie-backs with ears are the same length as the simple one, but they are about 6cm (2½in) wide when completed.

The length of the strip of material used to form the ruched tube depends on the type of material being used. When using chintz, I tend to cut the strips about 4 times the desired finished length. But silk requires about 6 times the final length of the tie-back to look sufficiently full.

The interlining is cut the same length as the finished tie-back and forms the core on to which the material is ruched.

If you want a thicker tie-back than the sample one, just make the tube wider. For a simple caterpillar tie-back, the interlining should always be cut 1½ times as wide as the tube material. For a caterpillar tie-back with ears, the interlining should be about 3½ times as wide as the finished width of the channel between the 'ears'.

Materials for caterpillar tie-backs

The materials for the caterpillar tie-backs are the same as for the plaited tie-backs, with the addition of contrasting material if you are making contrasting 'ears'.

Making simple caterpillar tie-backs

1 Cut a strip of material 12cm by 2.40m (4¾in by 7ft 10½in).

2 Make a single tube as described in steps 2 and 3 of the plaited tie-back.

3 Cut a strip of medium-weight interlining 17cm by 60cm (6¾in by 23½in).

4 Stuff the tube as in step 5 of the plaited tie-back (see page 100), but do not untie the string.

5 In order to ruche the material covering the interlining you must first secure the fabrics together at the opposite end from the string. Position the seam at the centre back, then machine stitch 1.5cm (½in) from the end of the tube through both tube and interlining.

6 Clamp the machine-stitched end on to the edge of the table. Holding the string firmly stretched out in one hand, ruche the tube on to the interlining (see diagram below) until it is pushed up just past the string knot. Undo the knot and slide the material back to line it up with the end of the

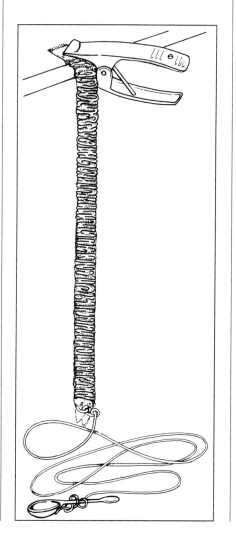

Caterpillar tie-back with ears

interlining. Machine stitch across this end as for the first end of the tie-back. Even up the gathers along the interlining.

7 Now bind the ends of the tie-back. Cut a piece of material 7.5cm by 6cm (2⅞in by 2in). Placing right sides and raw edges together, machine stitch one of the wider sides of this rectangle to one end of the tie-back, centring it so that 1.5cm (½in) extends to either

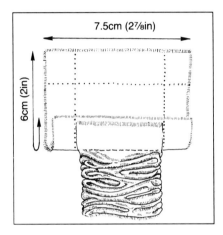

7.5cm (2⅞in)

6cm (2in)

side and working the stitches 1.5cm (½in) from the raw edges (see below). Turn under 1.5cm (½in) on the remaining raw edges, and fold it in half over the end of the tie-back. Hand sew it in place. Bind the other end of the tie-back in exactly the same way as the first.

8 Sew on rings as for the twisted tie-back. Make the second tie-back in the same way.

Making tie-backs with ears

1 Cut a strip of material 16cm by 2.40m (6¼in by 7ft 10½in).

2 Make the single tube as for the tubes in steps 2 and 3 for the plaited tie-back.

3 Place the seam at the centre back, then press the tube. Using matching thread, topstitch 1.5cm (½in) from one edge along the length of the tube. Topstitch along the other side of the

tube in the same way. This topstitching creates the stand-ups, or 'ears'.

4 Cut a strip of medium-weight interlining 12cm by 60cm (4¾in by 1ft 11½in).

5 Stuff the centre channel of the tube, as in step 5 of the plaited tie-back, but do not untie the string.

6 Follow steps 5–8 for the simple caterpillar tie-back to ruche the tube on to the interlining and bind the ends, but cut a rectangle 9.5cm by 6cm (3¾in by 2¼in) for the binding.

Making contrasting ears

1 Caterpillar tie-backs with contrasting ears are made in much the same way as those with plain ears, but the tubes are made differently to incorporate the contrasting colour. Cut two strips of main material 7cm by 2.40m (2¾in by 7ft 10½in). Cut two strips of contrasting material 5cm (2in) wide and the same length as the other strips.

2 Placing right sides and raw edges together, machine stitch one contrasting strip to one main strip along their long edges, making a 1.5cm (½in) seam. Stitch the other contrasting strip to the other edge of the main strip. Join the remaining strip of main material to the free edges of the contrasting strips to form a tube. Stitch a temporary seam across one end. Trim the seams to 8mm (¼in).

3 Follow step 3 for the plaited tie-back.

4 Align the seams so that the main strips are superimposed on top of one another, then press the tie-back flat. Using a matching thread, topstitch along the seamlines just inside both contrasting strips. This topstitching creates the contrasting stand-ups along the side edges.

5 Complete the tie-back as for the caterpillar with ears, steps 4–6, but cut a rectangle 10cm by 6cm (3¾in by 2in) for the binding.

BOW OR KNOT TIE-BACKS

To me, this type of tie-back fits in beautifully in any bedroom. I love their three-dimensional nature, and they are so soft in appearance. The great secret in making this tie-back is to make two separate sashes to tie around each curtain. So instead of constantly tying and untying it, you simply release one ring at the back. It is up to you how long to make the

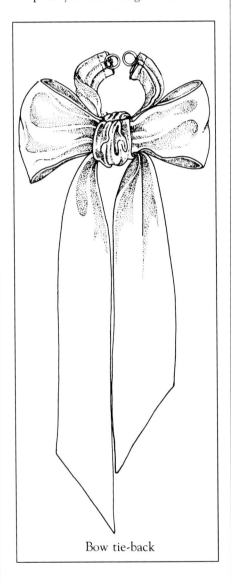

Bow tie-back

sashes. But my rule – LENGTH IS ELEGANCE – applies as always. The size of the sashes in the instructions is quite a good standard size.

All you need for this tie-back is a remnant of material. Interlining is not used, as it would hinder the crisp look of the finished bow and its knot.

Caterpillar tie-back

Making the bow tie-back

1 Cut two strips of material 22cm by 1.10m (8½in by 3ft 7in).

2 Fold one strip in half lengthways with right sides together. Beginning at the very end of the strip, machine stitch along the long side 1.5cm (½in) from the edge, ending 11cm (4¼in) from the other end; then turn the material 45 degrees and stitch diagonally to the fold, ending 1.5cm (½in) from the raw edge. Press to embed the stitches, trim the seam and turn the strip right side out. Turn in 1.5cm (½in) at the open end and hand sew the edges together. Press. Make the other sash in the same way.

3 At the straight end of one sash, make three or four pleats; machine stitch across them 1cm (¼in) from the end. Sew a ring to the pleated end (see diagram on previous page). Finish the

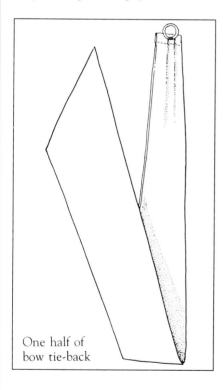

One half of bow tie-back

other sash in the same way. Then make two more sashes for the other tie-back.

4 Hook two sashes on to the tie-back hook at the side of the window, and bring them around the curtain. Tie the sashes together carefully. Do the same with the other tie-back.

ROSETTES AND BOWS

Flower rosettes, choux rosettes and bows have been used in window treatments for over two hundred years. The earliest type of pelmet was merely festooned material above the window. Bows or rosettes were stitched to the places where it was caught-up to form swags.

Where to use decorative details

It is important that you choose the right detail to complement exactly the inherent character of a window treatment. Rosettes, choux rosettes and bows are most often used in the following situations, where they make a significant contribution to the overall design of the window treatment:

– At the top two corners of an Austrian blind
– On a caught-up pelmet
– At the top centre of a pair of fixed-headed curtains
– On tie-backs

FLOWER ROSETTES

Flower rosettes have a lovely light and subtle quality. They are one of my favourite types of rosette. Made entirely by machine, they are particularly quick and easy both to make and to fix in place. They have the added advantage of a contrasting binding at

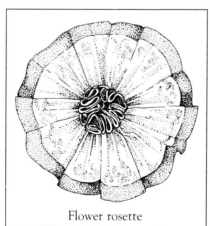

Flower rosette

both outer edge and centre. This is important if one is endeavouring to balance all the details of a particular window treatment which has a pelmet with a contrast-bound frill.

Size of finished flower rosettes

The flower rosette is made by gathering together a length of contrast-bound set-on frill (see page 21). The flower rosette used as the example in the following instructions is made from a frill with a finished width of 8cm (3in) – this is about as large as this type of rosette should be. You can, if you wish, make flower rosettes smaller than this, using a narrower frill; but, if you do, you should use a slightly narrower binding.

Materials for a flower rosette

All you will need to make a flower rosette is a small amount of your curtain material, matching thread and a contrasting material for the binding.

Making a flower rosette

1 Cut a strip of main material 8cm by 45cm (3in by 17¾in), using straight-edged scissors.

2 For the contrasting binding, cut two strips 4cm by 45cm (1½in by 17¾in), using pinking shears.

3 Place one contrasting strip on one edge of the main strips with right sides facing. Machine stitch them together 1cm (¼in) from the long edge. Stitch the other contrasting strip to the other edge of the main strip. Press to embed the stitches.

4 Follow steps **4**, **5** and **6** of the Contrast-bound set-on frill on page 21, but in step 6 do not fold under the beginning of the frill, and machine stitch just below the binding when gathering or pleating.

5 Placing right sides together, machine stitch the short ends of the frill together 1cm (¼in) from the edge. Trim the seam, but do not press it open. Work a machine zigzag along the raw edge.

6 Thread a large needle with a strong double thread and knot the end. With your fingertips, bunch together the gathered or pleated side of the frill just under the binding. Holding the rosette pinched together like this, insert the needle through the gathers just below the binding (see diagram next page) and pull the thread through. Now wrap the thread three times around the rosette, again just below the binding. Fasten off.

7 The rosette is basically finished – the gathered edge forms the flower centre and the rest the 'petals'. But to form it into its correct shape you must now close it like a flower, pulling the frill up over the gathered centre and pinching it together so that it is wrong side out. Wrap a rubber band tightly around the new gathers just below the outer binding (see diagram below). Leave the rubber band in place for a day. When the rubber band is removed, the rosette will curve forwards forming a flower-like shape.

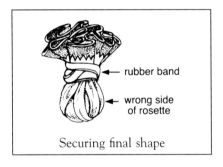

Securing final shape

8 To fix the finished flower rosette to a caught-up pelmet, sew it in place with a few hand stitches, or use a small tack which can be hammered into the pelmet board.

CHOUX ROSETTES

Choux rosettes have a particularly subtle and old-fashioned quality. Unlike flower rosettes, they are entirely hand sewn. The sample choux rosette in the following instructions is a good size for most requirements. It is 10cm (4in) in diameter. If you want to make a smaller choux rosette, simply make its circular base smaller, and cut a square of material with each side measuring 3 times the diameter of the circle.

Materials for a choux rosette

To make a choux rosette you will need a small amount of each of the following:

– Curtain material (and matching thread)
– Fusible buckram
– Medium-weight interlining

Making a choux rosette

1 Cut a circle of fusible buckram 10cm (4in) in diameter. Cut two pieces of

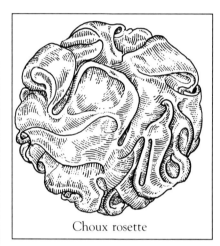

Choux rosette

medium-weight interlining exactly the same size and shape. Place the buckram between the two pieces of interlining and press to fuse them together. Divide the circle into quarters on one side by drawing two straight lines with a pencil through the centre (like dividing a cake). This will serve as a guide when gathering the material to the edge of the circle.

2 Cut a piece of material 30cm (12in) square.

3 You must now pleat the material on to the edge of the circular base, fitting one side of the material on to one quarter of the edge of the circle. Do not worry about making the pleats terribly regular. This does not matter at all, since they will not show when the choux is complete. (The choux will look much like a bathcap once the material is attached to the circle and before it is caught-down at random on the circle.)

To begin, thread a needle with a matching thread and knot the end. You will also need a thimble. Fold three small pleats along one edge of the material (right side upwards), beginning 2cm (¾in) from one

corner, working from left to right and about 1.5cm (½in) from the raw edge. Now with the three pleats in your right hand pick up the circle with your left hand so that the marked side of the circle is facing you. Fold the pleats over the edge of the circle, placing them at the beginning of one of the four sections and folding 1.5cm (½in) of the material to the back of the circle. Holding the pleats pinched over the edge of the circle with your left hand, insert the needle from back to front through the first pleat, above 5mm (¼in) from the edge. Pull the needle through and reinsert it a little to the right and from back to front.

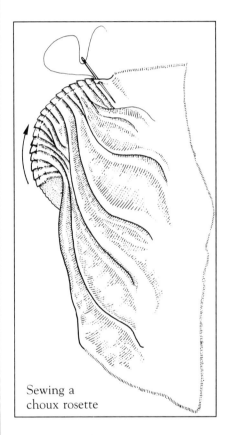

Sewing a choux rosette

Always working from left to right, work a few more stitches along the little pleats, making sure that the needle catches the circle with each stitch. Then with your right hand make a couple more pleats and fold them over the edge of the circle.

Choux rosettes add a finishing touch to the top of this grand, swagged half tester.

Holding the pleats in place with your left hand, stitch them to the circle.

Continue in this way, pleating the first side of the material on to the first quarter of the circle. Then pleat the next side of the square on to the next quarter of the circle, and so on. At the corners you will have to turn gradually on to the next side, starting about 2cm (¾in) from the corner. If, when pleating the fourth side, you have a little too much or too little material for the last quarter, this does not matter – just pleat it on to the circle as evenly as you can.

4 Once the material has been completely sewn to the edge of the circle, pull the material out over the edge all the way around. To pucker the material down on to the circular base (see below), use a matching thread and a thimble and catch it to the circle with a few stab stitches. You can choose to make either a rather 'explosive' and uncontrolled choux rosette, which is caught down in very few places, or a tighter and more methodically arranged one, entailing more stitches.

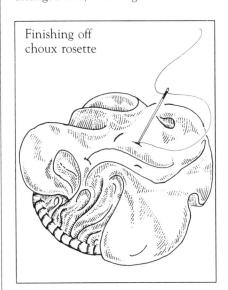

Finishing off
choux rosette

5 To cover the back of the choux rosette cut a circle of material 13cm (5in) in diameter. Place it on the back of the circle, turn under the edges and pin. Slip stitch around the edge, then remove the pins.

6 Fix it in place just as for the flower rosette.

BOWS

When making a bow for a window treatment I always make it from one long strip, which is simply tied to form a very natural bow. A bow made up artificially of three or four parts will always look unnatural. The size of the bow is a matter of personal preference.

Making the sash for the bow
1 Cut a strip of material 15cm by 1m (6in by 39in).

2 Fold the strip in half lengthways, placing right sides together. Starting at the centre of the long side, machine stitch 1.5cm (½in) from the edge, stopping 7.5cm (3in) from the end; then turn the material 45 degrees and stitch diagonally to the fold, ending 1.5cm (½in) from the raw edge. Leaving a gap about 10cm (4in) long at the centre (for turning the sash inside out), machine stitch the other end in the same way. Press to embed the

Bow

A bow creates a focus at the centre point of the kidney shape of a dressing table. The combination of the three-tiered skirt and the long sashes of the bow add up to a very soft, feminine effect.

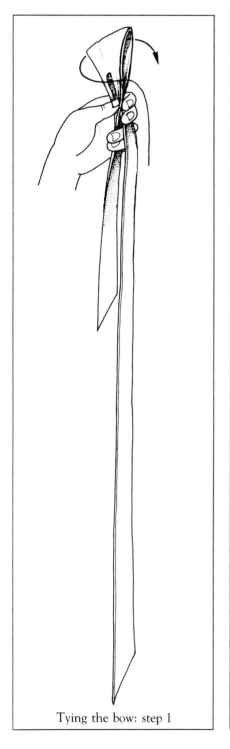

Tying the bow: step 1

stitches, trim the seam and turn the sash right side out.

3 Turn in the open edges, and hand sew them together. Press.

To tie the bow

1 Hold the sash with one-third of it folded down as shown left.

2 Wrap the longer section from right to left (see arrow in step 1) around the front of the top of the sash above your left hand, ending as shown below.

3 To form the left-hand loop of the bow, push the longer section through the 'knot' at the front as shown by the arrow in step 2.

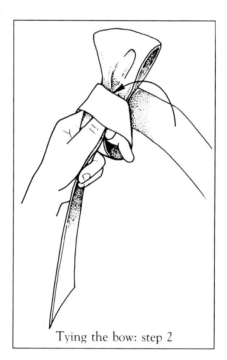

Tying the bow: step 2

4 Pull both loops of the bow from their back section to tighten the knot. If you pull from the front you will merely shorten the sash without tightening the knot. Arrange the ends of the sash so that both points fall on the inside (see finished bow on the facing page).

5 To attach the finished bow, either stitch it in place or staple the back section of each side of the bow to the pelmet board.

11

CORONAS, HALF TESTERS AND FOUR-POSTER BEDS

Coronas and half testers are the most elegant, beautiful things that can really enhance the general balance of a bedroom. The bed is a large, low, rectangular object that obviously dominates the room, and a corona or half tester can lift the eye to pretty detail above the bed. While the curtains on a four-poster bed are no longer needed for warmth, again they are an opportunity for soft decoration that adds both comfort and grandeur.

CORONA AND HALF TESTER DESIGN

It is best to totally tie the pelmet for any of these bed treatments in with the window pelmet. They should echo each other. For years, during the seventeenth and eighteenth centuries, four-poster beds were heavily curtained and pelmeted – long before anyone had got seriously into designing and hanging beautiful pelmets above the windows. So when pelmets became the 'in' thing many ideas for them naturally progressed from years of bed dressing. Now, however, when it comes to a corona, I would always do the window first and then the corona afterwards because, as always, I feel the window is the most important thing in the room, over and above anything else.

MAKING A CORONA

The height for a corona is slightly a matter of taste, and it will depend on your ceiling height, but an average height for a corona above the floor is between 2.3m and 2.7m (7ft 6in and 9ft) – but it is definitely up to you to decide. When it comes to the overall drop of the pelmet, it looks good if its drop (and, of course, its details) is exactly the same as the window pelmet. However, if your corona is placed not very high above the floor in comparison to your pelmet board (due to

the fact that you might possibly have a picture rail running around the room, for example) don't worry about feeling a need to reduce the dimensions of the corona pelmet by a few centimetres (or up to about 3in). It is most likely that your corona will be well below the height of the top of your window(s): it entirely depends on the height of your room.

Preparing the corona board

To construct a corona board you will need:

- Timber or blockboard approx 60cm × 48cm (2ft × 19in)
- Pair metal brackets 8cm × 5cm (3in × 2in)
- Screws for wall fixing: 5cm (2in), plus rawl plugs
- Screws for board fixing: 2cm (¾in)
- 25–28 4cm (1½in) brass screw eyes
- 130cm (4ft 6in) Velcro
- 60cm × 48cm (2ft × 19in) matching material
- Staple gun, drill
- Bradawl

1 Cut the board in the shape shown – like half an oval. (Make a paper template first, folded in half, to check you have the correct, even shape.)

2 Screw the brackets on to what will be the upper side of the board, 10cm (4in) from either edge.

3 Cover the underside of the board with matching fabric, using a staple

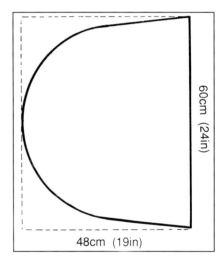

gun; pull it over the edge and staple round the edge. Trim off excess material.

4 Staple Velcro around the curved edge of the board.

5 Using a bradawl (spike) make holes in the timber (through the material) around the whole board, approx 1cm (½in) from the edge and 7cm (2½in) apart. Screw a screw eye into each hole.

An extraordinary, lavish four-poster, dressed with swags and tails and completed with a gathered, contrast-bound bed valance.

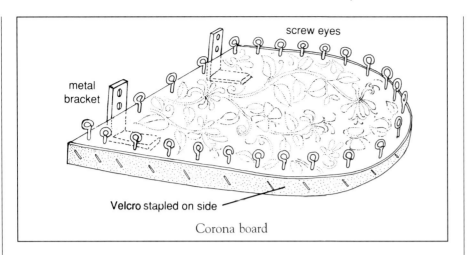

screw eyes

metal bracket

Velcro stapled on side

Corona board

Making the corona

You will need:

– 10.54m (11½yd) main (outer) material (plus five pattern repeats)
– 20.7m (22⅔yd) contrast (inner) material
– 10.54m (11½yd) medium weight interlining
– 5.1m (5⅔yd) sateen lining
– 4.2m (4⅔yd) narrow gathering tape
– 25–28 brass curtain hooks
– 2cm × 1cm (1in × ½in) wooden batten, same width as bed: 135cm (4ft 6in)
– 135cm (4ft 6in) Velcro
– Two brass roses to hold curtain at each side

Corona curtains: front

To hang these curtains, it is one of the few times you must use the narrow gathering tape, which I would rarely recommend but is absolutely correct for this situation. (The other situation you must use it in is with dressing table curtains and TV table curtains.)

The front corona curtains do not involve ordinary sateen lining material since it is essential to have the main fabric, or a lovely contrast, on both sides of the curtain, since the inside as well as the outside is permanently visible. Interlining is essential for that thick, sumptuous look in the curtains around the front of the corona; but is not sewn into the back curtain, behind the headboard.

Bed size, standard double: 188cm × 135cm (6ft 2in × 4ft 6in)

1 Measure the curved front of corona board. For the dimensions given here, the curve measures 128cm (4ft 2½in).

2 Cut material 3.02m (9ft 11in) long by 1½ widths wide. Cut contrast material for inner curtain the same size. (I thoroughly recommend a contrast since the effect is beautiful.) Cut interlining exactly the same size. Do this for each front curtain.

3 For each front curtain, place the outer and inner material right sides together, with raw edges together, at the top. Machine stitch along the top with a 1.5cm (½in) seam allowance. Press and trim seam.

4 Clamp curtains on to your work table, outer curtain face down, and lift away the back curtain so it hangs on to the floor, so that you have the wrong side of the outer curtain facing you. Place interlining on curtain with raw edges level along their longest sides. At the top, make sure the raw edge is level with the machined seam. Clamp securely.

5 On the interlining, draw a line (with a pen) 6cm (2½in) below the machine line at the top of the curtain. Pin the interlining through to the outer material so it cannot move away. Now machine stitch this through to the front, stitching along your pen line, but you must stop machine stitches 5cm (2in) from either end. This is essential so that you can turn in your interlining at the next stage. Trim away interlining to approx 1cm (⅜in) above the machine line.

6 Fold the interlining back down the leading edge of the curtain, to leave a 5cm (2in) gap on the main material – between its raw edge and the fold of the interlining. Interlock the fold of the interlining to the main material

(see steps 9–13, pages 44–5) but stop the interlocking stitches 20cm (8in) before the bottom of curtain.

7 At the leading edge, fold the main material over the interlining and clamp (no need to pin). Now do pyramid stitches (see page 70) over the raw edges of the main material and bump, going through the bump, but not through to the front of the main material. Again, stop stitches 20cm (8in) before the bottom of the curtain.

8 Swivel curtain so that the hem is running along the long side of the table. Clamp. Turn up 12cm (5in) for the hem.

9 Fold the inner curtain material from the floor, so that it is lying exactly on top of the interlined curtain. Carefully fold in its leading edge so that it meets exactly with the edge of the fold of the outer material. Pin. Slip stitch invisibly.

10 Stop stitches 12cm (5in) before the hem so that you can do a neat right angle (to exactly mirror the one which is already stitched at the corner of the curtain). Pin and slip stitch.

11 Swivel the curtain again and clamp so you can slip stitch along the hem, with the folds of the outer curtain and the fold of the inner material exactly level. Repeat steps 9 and 10 on the other long side of the curtain. I thoroughly recommend working from the top downwards in this situation, in case you gain any excess, for some reason or other. This, if necessary, can be easily lost in the turn-up of the hem. You may feel you want to press the edges of the curtain with an iron. On the other hand the look is lovely when the edges of the curtain do not look all pressed and flat – but rounded and thick instead.

12 Mark a line with a pen, 4cm (1½in) below top of curtain on the outer material at its front. Machine stitch narrow gathering tape in position so that

The corona and windows use pelmets with a serpent-shaped, gathered skirt off a buckram-interfaced band. Fixing the pelmets at exactly the same height, and the soft, complementary colours both help to create an atmosphere of restful comfort.

The colour of this corona's back curtain is carefully repeated in the knotted rope on its goblet-pleated pelmet.

the top of the tape is level with the pen line. There is no need to pin this first unless you feel nervous about it. Feeding it straight on is very easy.

13 Pull up the cord until the width of the top of the curtain measures 61cm (24½in). (This allows for a small gap in the centre of the corona, between the two front curtains.) Knot cords and roll up spare string and stitch to secure at top. (This is purely for neatness. You could cut this excess string off but it is quite a good idea to retain it to leave you the option of altering the curtains for another situation one day.) Place a brass curtain hook in the tape every 7cm (2¾in) approx, to correspond with the screw eyes on the corona board.

Repeat all steps for the second front curtain.

Corona curtain: back

You obviously want the back curtain to be made of the same material as that lining the back of your front curtains. You want the fullness of this single curtain to be at least four times the width of the back of the corona board: 60cm (2ft). The reason for this is that the curtain must be able to stretch out easily across the width of the bed, at the skirting board; you fix the lower edge of this back-curtain with Velcro on to a batten.

1 Cut two widths of inner material: 2.54m (8ft 4in). Cut (sateen) lining the same. Do not use any interlining since its bulk would prevent you from being able to pull it up to the fullness necessary.

2 Make two fabric loops about 10cm (4in) long and 1.5cm (½in) wide, from the back curtain material. These will eventually loop around the shaft of the brass roses to hold the curtain out to the correct width.

3 You can entirely machine stitch this curtain – very unusual in purist curtain making. Clamp chintz and lining to the table – right sides together. Pin around the two sides and the hem. Pin the loops into the side seams 1.28m (4ft 2in) from the bottom.

4 Machine stitch with a 1.5cm (½in) seam allowance all around the three sides taking care to stitch the loops in. Trim seams back to 1cm (½in), especially in the corners. Turn and press.

5 Clamp the top of the curtain along the table, right sides down. Turn in the two remaining raw edges, and pin them vertically with the pin heads above the folds of the material.

6 Sew on narrow gathering tape with the same stand-up as on the front of the curtains.

7 Cut a strip of soft Velcro the same width as your bed, and machine stitch it on to the very bottom of this curtain on the lining side. It is fine for the machine stitches to come through to the front of the curtain. These stitches are irrelevant since they will be totally hidden from view behind the bed base. However, the bottom of this back curtain will be considerably wider than the width of a standard double bed, so you need to take tucks in the curtain as you stitch it on to the Velcro. Place hooks in the pulled-up tape of the back curtain to correspond with the screw eyes in the corona board.

Hanging the corona board

1 Hold the corona board against wall and mark with a pen a short line to indicate the position of the underside of the board. Also, mark the holes in the brackets against the wall so you know where to drill for the screws. In this case, the corona board should be 2.73m (9ft) from the floor to the bottom of the board.

2 Drill two holes for each bracket and plug with a rawl plug.

3 Cut the 1cm × 2cm (½in × 1in) batten the exact width of the bed. Screw this into the wall behind the bed with it resting exactly on top of the skirting board.

4 Staple the strip of hard Velcro on to the batten with your staple gun.

5 Using 3cm (1¼in)-long screws, attach corona board to the wall. This is no easy feat. You need one person to hold and steady the board in place

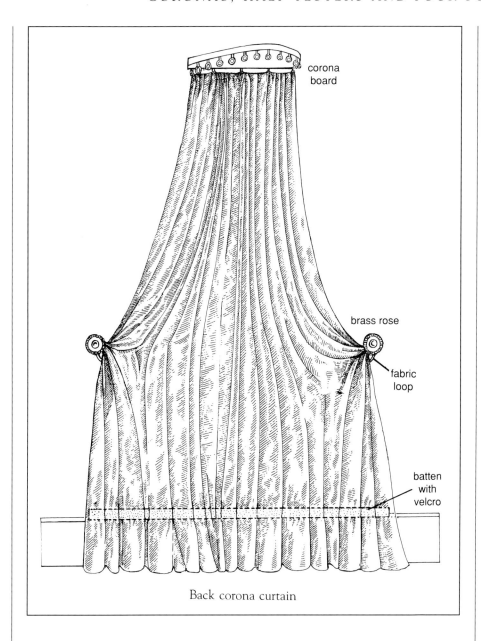

corona board

brass rose

fabric loop

batten with velcro

Back corona curtain

while another person screws the screws in place.

6 Hang the back curtain from the board, slipping its hooks into the screw eyes.

7 Pull the bottom of the back curtain taut from the centre while feeding its Velcroed lower edge on to the Velcro on the batten.

8 Now hang the pair of front curtains. You want the pair not to meet in the centre of the corona but to stop approx 7cm (3in) apart. Place brass roses 1.28m (4ft 2in) above the floor, screwing them in through the loops on the back curtain.

Corona pelmet

There are many different styles of pelmet you can use on this corona – all of which could look wonderful in a bedroom, especially when it echoes the window pelmet. All the following headings are highly suitable:

– Pencil-pleated (page 82)
– Deep pencil-pleated
– Goblet-pleated (page 83)
– Smocked (eight different stitches) (page 86)
– Fusible buckram and gathered skirt (page 90)
– Pleated stand-up on Velcro (page 89)
– Gathered stand-up on Velcro (page 89)

All these are made in exactly the same way as an ordinary pelmet, and are fixed on to the curved front of the corona board with Velcro. Check the specific instructions for the amount of material needed (2, 2½ or 3 times round the front of the board).

HALF TESTERS

Half testers are constructed in exactly the same way as coronas, except that the board from which they hang is rectangular, instead of curved.

The board should be the same width as your bed, and about 50cm (19½in) deep (from the wall to the outer edge). It should be fixed the same distance from the floor as a corona board (see page 108). Rather than stapling plain material to the board's underside, pleat it first (so that the pleats run in the head-to-foot direction), in the same way as for a four-poster ceiling (see page 115).

To calculate the measurements of the curtains you must measure around the two sides and the front of the board, and allow 2½ times this distance. For the back curtain, you need approx 2 times the width of the bed.

Obviously the half-tester pelmet should extend around three sides of the board. All styles of pelmet look good on a half tester.

FOUR-POSTER BEDS

Four-poster beds are wonderfully cosy and secure to sleep in. This style of bed is hundreds of years old, and every type of person has been sleeping in them for centuries – from kings and queens downwards.

Nowadays there is something very grand about a four-poster, but they were originally designed to serve a practical purpose in terms of warmth. With poor glazing, inadequate curtains and no central heating, bedrooms were notoriously cold, so to be high off the floor and snugly tucked in behind drawn curtains was essential. Now, apart from the occasional freezing cold house in northern Britain, the need to create warmth behind tightly closed curtains is superfluous due to efficient central heating and improved insulation. However, four-posters are still highly popular since they are a wonderful excuse to be

The half tester in this room has great impact, due to the strong contrast of its back curtain, and as the window treatment is a softer, Austrian blind.

highly decorative with the most significant piece of furniture in the room.

If your bedroom is especially large or has a particularly high ceiling, this type of bed is a brilliant way of making the room feel smaller and cosier, and indeed of 'bringing the ceiling down'. In terms of the inherent balance of the room, to elevate some of that huge rectangular shape dominating the room is a good way of achieving a better overall balance in the room as a whole.

Do take a very careful look at your bedroom before you embark on such a project: it is essential that the room is large enough to take a four-poster.

The sample four-poster

The beautiful, dressed four-poster (right) is supremely elegant. It looks inviting and comfortable, and the colours are delightfully soft for a bedroom, blending easily with the accompanying wallpaper and furniture.

Pelmet

This has pretty rhythmical lines with some of my favourite details like a stand-up heading on Velcro, finished off with rope and rosettes. The lower edge has a set-on two-tone fringe with a fan-edged top. This trimming perfectly accentuates the lovely curves in the lower edge of the pelmet.

1 Measure around three sides of the top of the four-poster (excluding the head end).

Sample bed size: 1.98m × 1.55cm (6ft 6in × 5ft 1in)

Total distance round bed: 5.51m (18ft 1in). Multiply this by three since for a stand-up heading gathered into Velcro you will need approx 3 times that amount.

2 Cut approx 16.73m (18yd 1ft): 5.51m × 3 + 20cm for seams: 12 widths approx. If you are using patterned material you must allow for twelve pattern repeats. Your cutting length should be 70cm (28in). Unfortunately you will have some wastage here since you have to start the whole bed pelmet with the maximum length necessary and then cut your curves. You are aiming for a finished drop, at the lowest points by the uprights of 65cm (25½in) and then your highest drop, when it goes completely straight, should be approx 45cm (17¾in).

3 Fold joined material in half and start marking out shape from the central fold. This is just as if you were plotting the shape of an ordinary serpent-tailed pelmet (page 97). If the width of the bed is 155cm (5ft 1in) you have got a total of 4.65m (5yd) allowed for this, but your material is folded in half so it is 2.33m (2½yd) approx and you have got 5.74m (6yd 10in) allowed for each side. Use the diagram below to guide you. Obviously, the material is so long you can't lay out all the material at once. Work in sections, bearing in mind the overall shape.

4 Machine stitch the fringe to the outer material. It is vital to attach it at this stage rather than later to avoid ugly machine stitches at the back, visible when you are lying in the bed.

5 Now follow the steps for a Velcro-headed pelmet (see page 89): start by machine stitching the inner and outer layers at the lower edge, right sides together.

6 When the pelmet is completed, hand sew the rope over the Velcro heading and then make choux rosettes

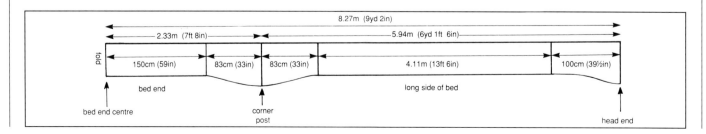

114

(page 104). Fix the pelmet on by stapling Velcro on to a batten below the bed ceiling frame or on to an existing ridge (or use self-adhesive Velcro if you are worried about damaging your antique).

Curtains

1 Make one pair of curtains like front corona curtains (page 110) for the sides at the head end, and hang them like the corona curtains using brass screw eyes and narrow gathering tape.

2 Make a single curtain like the back corona curtain, to run along the back, and hang it on Velcro or 4cm (1½in) brass screw eyes, like a corona.

Valance

Make a gathered bed valance (page 34) to fit the bed. Make two extra, separate bits of skirt, 15cm (6in) when gathered up. Fold in the raw edges at the top. Machine gather (page 18). Sew a popper on at each corner and then one either side of the corner of the valance so the extra skirt will now fit round the upright.

Ceiling

1 Have made, in blockboard or timber, a piece of wood to fit the ceiling of the four-poster.

2 Cut enough material to make a pleated ceiling. You will have to seam

The curved lines of this four-poster pelmet softens the dark wood and hard lines of the frame. The two-tone fringe adds a definite line, and the tassels lead the eye down to the bed itself.

join, but do not have it in the centre – as with curtains or a bedcover. You will need three to four widths, cut approx 2.08m (6ft 10in) long.

3 Machine pleat one end on the sewing machine. Staple this end on to the timber at the head end. Then fold pleats along the other end to correspond with those already there; staple each pleat as you go.

12

CHILDREN'S BEDROOMS

A child's room should look as inviting and cosy as possible, as it is the central point, and the only really personal space, of his or her life. The requirements are more practical than in an adult's bedroom: storage for toys as well as clothes, space for play and perhaps for a desk. It is important to bear these needs in mind when planning the furnishings, as well as creating a sympathetic environment in which to play and sleep.

DESIGNING FOR CHILDREN

If you have designed your child's bedroom correctly, he or she will want to spend hours playing in there (with or without friends), or peacefully reading a book, or listening to tapes – mine all certainly do.

If you think about it, the last thing he will do at night (certainly in the summer) and the first thing he will do in the morning is look at his curtains. Therefore they are a very important factor in the room and I deeply disapprove of ever lining them in 'blackout' material. To wake up in a blacked-out room is a weird, disorienting experience. I will never forget my yellow hammer birds flying through their apple blossom: it was such a happy experience on a daily basis. So if you are worrying about keeping your child asleep by darkening the room until he/she drops the temporary early-morning waking habit, simply install a very dark (blue, red or green) roller blind. This can serve a useful purpose while there is a problem, yet when the problem subsides, the blind can happily become redundant.

There are two primary considerations for children's rooms. First, do not make your window treatment in any way babyish. It is very easy to be tempted to buy chintz covered in darling bunnies and birds when you are pregnant but, in a second, the baby has grown up to be a huge eight-year-old boy who would far rather

have tartans, stripes or far more 'grown-up' abstract trains, boats or sheep. To channel all your money and energy into materials that will be outgrown after a few years is such a waste of time.

Second, from a practical point of view your window treatment should involve as little space loss as possible. Space under the window sill is brilliant for toy boxes, book shelves, a desk or merely carefully arranged dolls, cars, Red Indian camps, or soldier battles, etc. So, the obvious thing is to have lovely floor-length curtains and a beautiful pelmet, but to have a blind as well (an Austrian blind for a girl or a roller blind for a boy). Therefore, the long curtains do not have to be used, yet the night can be shut out.

GOBLET-PLEATED PELMET WITH RABBITS

Putting little furry rabbits or teddies (about 12cm or 5in high) in the goblet pleats of a pelmet (see page 83) is the most adorable idea for a pelmet in a child's bedroom. Sadly all my children's windows are long since done. I long to find an excuse to incorporate this particular pelmet somewhere at home. This is a versatile idea as well, because when you feel the child is too old to have rabbits in the goblet pleats, you can merely remove them and either leave the pleats empty or

replace the animals with a contrast colour exploding out.

This design of goblet pelmet looks particularly good if you contrast bind the top and bottom of the pelmet with 1cm (½in) of contrast colour.

Making the pelmet

Follow all instructions for a goblet-pleated pelmet (see page 83). Make sure you contrast bind the pelmet with 1cm (⅜in) showing at both its top and bottom (see below). This contrast is slightly a question of taste, and you may feel you want to leave out either the top binding or the bottom.

I feel that the rabbits are a major feature and therefore must be pronounced and set off in a very important way. It is the contrast lines, and most especially the top one, that will do this. When you order your contrast, remember to order enough for the day when eventually you will remove the bunnies or teddies and replace them with the explosive, contrast-matching colour. You obviously need to keep the material for this safely put away – it is so easy to forget where you have stored it when the day comes.

An Austrian blind is ideal in this busy and obviously well-used child's room, as it gives the room some softer lines, and leaves plenty of space underneath for the bunk bed.

AUSTRIAN BLINDS

Austrian blinds are very beautiful in girls' (and adults') bedrooms as they are so feminine and curvaceous. They can have an enormous variety of headings: pencil pleats (page 73), shallow or deep; goblet pleats (page 83); smocked – any of the eight varieties listed (page 86); stand-up heading on Velcro, gathered or pleated (page 89).

On their own they are fine but, even better, they can be used in an overall window treatment as an extra dimension as well as the lovely thick curtains and an elegant pelmet.

LEFT *Any stuffed animal can be used to create a delightful detail for a child's goblet-pleated pelmet.*

BELOW *As there is no housing space next to this eave window, an Austrian blind is a perfect window treatment.*

For the bunnies or teddies to fit comfortably into a goblet pleat, make the pleats 12–14cm (4¾–5½in) wide. You want them to fit snugly but not tightly – basically, so that their little armpits rest on the top of the pleat. You will need four to five bunnies or teddies per width in the pelmet (depending whether the material is 1.20m (48in) or 1.40m (56in) wide).

Contrast binding

Cut strips of 7cm (3in) wide and as long as all your widths, joined up, requires. When you purchase the bunnies or teddies, it is quite likely they may have tiny bows around the necks. It is tempting to replace the bows with other ones, in a matching/contrasting colour to your pelmet. I would strongly advise you to do none of this. The bunnies and teddies definitely look best with bare necks; sitting in their goblet pleats, above a contrast line, they look brilliant, whereas extra neck bows look fussy and overdone. The bunnies look particularly good due to the height of their ears which balances the drop of the pelmet very well.

Suitable materials

Choose your material with care – either to blend, or to contrast, or merely to create privacy. Chintz is particularly fitting for bedrooms and especially for Austrian blinds as it has got so much bounce and body. Its fundamental nature allows it to behave very well in the form of an Austrian blind.

Blinds made in thin, white, unlined silk or spotted muslin work very well when both privacy and maximum light are priorities.

On the other hand be careful not to overdo the feminine atmosphere in the bedroom. If many other items – bed valance, corona, dressing table and chairs – are all very gathered and frilled, an Austrian blind may be totally over the top. It's up to you to decide whether your room can take this added sumptuous detail.

Austrian blinds in bathrooms

Austrian blinds are often the perfect design for a bathroom window. You are bound to have a radiator under the window. You particularly want maximum heat and total privacy in your bathroom, so an Austrian blind is perfect. As well, there are often units below bathroom windows so floor-length curtains are sadly impossible. From a practical point of view it is useful to be able to pull Austrian blinds up high, to avoid splashes.

Finished drop

An Austrian blind is hung from a batten 5cm by 2.5cm (2in by 1in). The batten is fixed to the wall just above the window architrave, with the 5cm (2in) side flush with the wall. Alternatively the batten can be fixed to the top of the architrave itself, level with its top.

The blind is hung from the batten with Velcro, so to determine the finished drop required for your Austrian blind you must measure from the top of the batten position to just below the window-sill.

Keep in mind that these blinds take up one third of the window space when pulled up and will therefore obscure some of the light coming in the window. If you wish, you can overcome this drawback by fixing the batten well above the architrave to create extra height.

Finished flat blind

When completely closed, the blind must never have a straight lower edge, but must have definite curves created by the swags of the blind. This means that the blind is gathered vertically at the lower edge even when closed, and the finished flat length of the blind is longer than the finished drop of the gathered hanging blind. The amount of extra material needed to ensure this effect is about 30cm (12in).

Width of the blind before pleating

You can use pencil pleating for the heading of the blind. It requires a finished flat blind width at least 2½ times the width of the window. The pencil pleats would not be full enough without this amount of material.

You can also make the blind when it is only about twice the width of the window before pleating.

Width of the blind after pleating

The width of the blind after pleating is, of course, determined by the width of the batten. The batten should extend past the architrave by 2cm (¾in) on each side. The finished pleated blind should then extend a little past the ends of the batten so that the batten is obscured sufficiently from view. If your blind has, however, a frill along three sides, the finished blind itself should be pleated to the exact width of the batten. The frill will then extend past the batten on either side to hide it.

Handmade frills

If the blind is to be set in a recess, only the lower edge should have a frill. Any vertical frills on a blind set in a recess would be likely to rub against the adjacent walls when being opened and closed and would look too cramped in the narrow space. However, in other situations a blind looks wonderful with a frill along three sides (see page 18 for Machine-gathered frills).

The sample blind

The blind used as the example in the instructions has a pencil-pleated heading and a frill around the remaining three sides.

Austrian blinds also work well in bathrooms, especially when clearance is needed over a central-heating radiator.

The finished drop of the sample blind and the batten width are as follows:

– Finished blind drop 1.80m (5ft 11in)
– Batten width 1.30m (4ft 3¼in)

To calculate the cutting length, add the hem allowance, the turn-down allowance at the top for pencil pleats (see page 73) and the excess for swags to the finished drop:

Finished drop	180cm	(5ft 11in)
Turn-down	10cm	(4in)
Hem allowance	1.5cm	(½in)
Swags excess	30cm	(12in)
Cutting length	221.5cm	(7ft 3½in)

The finished flat drop is calculated by adding the finished drop and the length of the swags excess, which in this case adds up to a total of 210cm (6ft 11in).

For this particular window treatment you should use two widths of curtain material. It does not matter whether the width of the material from selvedge to selvedge is 120cm (47in) or 137cm (54in); two widths will be adequate since together they are roughly twice the width of the batten.

When buying material, remember to add the length of the pattern repeat to each of the widths to be cut, so that you have an allowance for pattern-matching (see page 17).

The number of swags chosen for the sample blind is three, which is highly recommended for this particular width. Too many swags will make the design look too fussy and it will lose much of its elegance.

Lining

Austrian blinds are not interlined, as they must be essentially light and bouncy. For pencil-pleat and goblet-pleat headings, however, you will need a strip of medium-weight interlining to insert from edge to edge of the top of the blind, along the heading. When using fusible buckram in a heading it is essential to place interlining between the buckram and the main material. But with pencil-pleat tape the interlining is used merely to enhance the look of the heading by giving it far more body and depth.

The interlining should be the same depth as the chosen type of heading. The sample blind has a pencil-pleated heading, so it requires a strip of interlining the same depth as the gathering tape – or in this case 8cm (3in).

The amount of lining required for an Austrian blind is 15cm (6in) less than the amount of main material.

Making the blind

1 Cut the widths for the blind. The widths must be joined in the same way as for pelmets – that is with no seam running up the centre. So if you are using only two widths of material you will have to cut one of the widths in half lengthways and sew a half-width to either side of the whole width. Pattern-join the widths (see page 17). Cut and join the lining in the same way. Press all seams to embed the machine stitches, then press the seams open.

2 Make an inset frill long enough to go along the two sides and the lower edge of the blind (see *Machine-gathered frills*, page 18).

3 Placing the beginning and the end of the frill 18cm (7in) from the top edge, pin the frill to the main material around three sides, with right sides and raw edges together. This allows for the 18cm (7in) heading allowance at the top of the blind. Machine stitch the frill to the blind material 1.5cm (½in) from the raw edge, removing the pins as you stitch. Then lay the material wrong side down on the table. Keeping the frill lying towards the centre of the material, use a few pins to secure the corners in place flat against the blind. This is done as a safeguard to ensure that the frill does not catch at the corners when the lining is machine stitched over it.

4 With the blind material still facing upwards on the table, lay the lining on top of it, right sides and raw edges together. Pin the lining in place around the previously stitched sides. Turn the blind over so that the main material is facing upwards, and machine stitch the lining to the blind material, working the stitches just inside the first row and again beginning and ending 18cm (7in) from the top. This stitching is worked inside the first line in order to conceal the first line when the blind is turned right side out. Press to embed the stitches. Trim the seam allowance to about 5mm (¼in). Turn the blind right side out and press the seam flat.

5 Clamp the lower edge of the blind wrong side up on to one long edge of the table. Holding the top of the blind stretched from the clamps, pull firmly on both fabric layers to take out the slack. Insert a few pins around the blind so that the layers will remain together.

Making the heading

1 Keeping the blind wrong side up, turn it so that it is lying lengthways on the table. Remembering that the finished flat drop includes the swags excess, measure the finished flat drop up from the bottom of the blind. Measure, mark and join the marks along the top of the blind as described in step 1 on page 73. Then cut *the lining only* along the line just drawn.

2 Turn the chintz (which will measure 8cm (3in) approx) over this raw edge of lining and pin with pin heads uppermost. Machine stitch on, as for the curtain heading described on page 74. However, sew on Velcro at top instead of inserting hooks.

The vertical gathers

Before the tape is pulled up the plastic rings should be sewn on to the back of the blind. The finished blind is gathered vertically (at the back) with cords, which are held in place by these plastic rings. You should use rings no more than 1.5cm (½in) in diameter.

Sewing on plastic rings

1 When sewing the rings to the back of the blind, use a thread that matches the blind material, and stitch right through both the lining and the blind material. Do not worry that the stitches will show on the front; they are well hidden due to the design of the blind.

Beginning at the lower edge, sew rings to the wrong side of the blind along one side edge, spacing them about 15cm (6in) apart and placing the last ring 25cm (10in) from the top of the blind (the rings have to stop clear of the heading so as not to interfere with it). The sample blind would therefore have about 14 rings along the side edge. Only the rings on the lower edge will receive much pressure. The other plastic rings are there purely to guide the cords, so you need not sew them on as conscientiously as you sew on the ones on the lower edge.

Back of Austrian blind

2 Sew rings along the other side edge in corresponding positions.

3 With the blind clamped to the table wrong side up, divide the lower edge into three sections in order to mark the positions of two more vertical rows of rings. Using the long folding ruler as a guide to ensure straight lines, sew on two more vertical rows of rings in positions corresponding to the rings at the side edges. When the blind is eventually pulled up on cords threaded

through these four lines of rings, three swags will form.

Hanging the blind

1 Before the batten is fixed to the wall it must be properly prepared. The batten is eventually fixed in place so that one of the 5cm (2in) sides is flush with the wall. (See page 119 for the width of the batten across top of window.) To prepare the batten, first cover it with a piece of the main material, using a staple gun. This is a profes-

sional touch which will ensure that if the batten is ever visible it will not be conspicuous. Then staple a strip of stiff 2cm (¾in)-wide Velcro across the 5cm (2in)-deep front of the batten (along the top edge).

2 With a bradawl, make holes at each end of the batten to correspond to the rings at the side edges of the blind. Screw a 4cm (1½in)-long screw eye into each of these holes. Divide the space between these two eyes by three, and insert two more screw eyes in the same way. The positions of these screw eyes will correspond to the positions of the other two rows of rings on the blind.

3 Drill a hole at each end of the batten from front to back. The batten is now ready to be fixed to the wall with a screw placed through each of these holes. You would be well advised to have a professional fix the batten in place to ensure that it is securely attached.

4 Once the batten is securely in place, hang the blind from the Velcro. Cut four pieces of strong nylon blind cord 4m (4½yd) long (they will be trimmed later). Tie one end of the first length of cord to the ring on the left side of the lowest channel. Feed the cord through the rings along this side of the blind, then through all four screw eyes on the underside of the batten. Tie the next length of cord to the next ring on the lowest channel, and feed the cord through the rings on that part of the blind, but threading it through three screw eyes on the right side of the batten. Continue in this way for the remaining two sets of rings.

5 In order to ensure that the blind does not sag into the window recess and that the lower edge – even though swagged – will remain parallel to the window-sill, attach a length of dowelling to the rings along the lower edge of the blind. You will need a wooden dowelling rod 1.5cm (½in) in diameter and the same length as the batten, which means, in the case of the sample blind, 1.30m (4ft 3¼in). Cut a strip of lining 10cm by 133cm (4in by 4ft 4¼in). Turn under 1.5cm (½in) at both short ends and press. Then turn under 1.5cm (½in) along both long sides and press. Place wrong sides and folded edges together, and machine stitch close to the fold and across one short end. Sew four plastic rings to the seamed edge of the tube, one at each end and the other two evenly spaced between. Slide the rod into the fabric tube, then hand sew the opening together. Now tie the rings along the lower edge of the blind to the rings on the covered rod. Do not trim the ends of the cord, but tie them up instead, so that you can later untie these knots to remove the blind for cleaning. Never hang an Austrian blind without a rod tied in place.

6 Pull the strings to adjust them, so that the rod at the lower edge of the blind is level and the blind is fully down. Remember that when it is down, the lower edge must still be swagged and the drop of the blind should come to just below the sill. With the blind closed in this position, cut the four cords so that about 15cm (6in) of each cord remains below the last screw eye. Knot these ends to one end of a 5cm (2in) S-hook. Sew through the knot to ensure that it will not come undone. Attach a decorative bell-pull rope with a tassel to the other end of the S-hook. When the blind is pulled up, the rope is wrapped around a brass cleat attached to the architrave.

Cleaning the blind
When the blind needs cleaning, simply untie the cords at the lower edge and then remove the blind. Leave the cord in place for the blind's return.

Glossary

The following list of terms includes some British words that may not be familiar to American readers.

Austrian blind – British term (American 'Austrian shade' or 'balloon shade') – a single curtain that is gathered horizontally across the heading, and as it is pulled up, is also gathered vertically

bed valance – British term for a U.S. 'dust ruffle' – a skirt which covers a bed base, from the bottom of the mattress to the floor

blockboard – thick plywood, about 1.5cm (½in) thick

brass rose – hardware fixture for holding back curtains, especially corona curtains

bullion – a thick, twisted fringe

bump – a fairly thick British fabric, similar to American 'table felt' or 'reinforced felt', made of cotton and used to interline curtains

chipboard – particle board

curtains – term used in Britain to include all soft fabric window dressing (apart from blinds/shades), including some that in the United States would be called 'draperies'

domette – a soft, fleecy British fabric, similar to American Thermo Lamb, made of a brushed cotton and used as a lightweight interlining for curtains

fusible buckram – a stiff, firm interfacing fabric used to stiffen the headings of curtains and pelmets. If you cannot find fusible buckram, an alternative is to use ordinary buckram and fuse it in place with a strip of fusing web

goblet pleat – British term for American 'French pleat'

housing space – British term (American 'stackback') – the area to either side of a window required to accommodate the curtains when fully open

leading edges – the centre vertical edges of a pair of curtains

net curtain – British term for American 'glass curtain'

overlap arm – the part of a pulley system to which is attached the leading edge of the curtain that will overlap the other edge slightly when the curtains are closed. This and the other arm of the system are called the 'master slides'

pelmet – British term for both American 'valance' and 'cornice'

pelmet board – British term (American 'valance shelf') – a horizontally fixed piece of wood from which a pelmet is hung

pencil pleats – British term (American 'shirred heading') – narrow, closely spaced pleats

piping – British term (American 'cording' or 'welting') – fabric-covered cord inserted in a seam as a decorative accent

pulley system – British term for the mechanism of cords and sliders used on some curtain rails to enable the curtains to be opened and closed mechanically; in the United States, a rail of this type is called 'traverse rod'

rawl plugs – known in America as wall plugs or lag shields: used when fixing screws into cement or brick walls to give screws something to grip

roller blind – British term for the American 'window shade' or 'roller shade'

Suppliers

Materials and equipment for soft furnishings are available in a wide range of shops, but the following list of suppliers will be especially useful for both the professional and the home sewer.

TABLE CLAMPS AND FOLDING RULERS

U.K.
Lady Caroline Wrey
60 The Chase,
London SW4 0NH
Tel: 071 622 6625

U.S.A.
Greentext Upholstery Supplies,
Tel: 212 206 8585

LADDERS, TIMBER, STAPLE GUNS, SCREWS

U.K.
Any good timber merchant, DIY shop or ironmonger

U.S.A.
Duo-Fast
20 Corporate Drive,
Orangeburg, NY 10962
Tel: 914-365-2400

Any local lumberyard or hardware store

INTERLININGS AND LININGS

U.K.
Hesse and Co
Waring and Gillow Estate,
Western Avenue,
London W3 0TA
Tel: 081 992 2212
Fax: 081 752 0012

Hunter and Hyland Ltd (see *Curtain-hanging materials*)

Porter Nicholson
Portland House,
Norlington Road,
London EC10 6JX
Tel: 081 539 6106
Fax: 081 558 9200

U.S.A.
Gige Interiors, Ltd (see *Curtain-hanging materials*)

Local fabric and sewing stores

SEWING EQUIPMENT
Including the following: needles, pins, metal buttons, stranded embroidery floss, threads, tape measures, scissors.

U.K.
John Lewis Partnership (all branches),
278-306 Oxford Street,
London W1A 1EX
Tel: 071 629 7711
Fax: 071 629 0849

Any good haberdashery department

U.S.A.
Calico Corners
745 Lancaster Pike
Strafford,
Wayne, PA 19087
Tel: 215-688-1505 (national chain)

Any good notions departments or local fabric stores

PLAIN COLOURED CHINTZES (AND OTHER MATERIALS)

U.K.
Hallis and Hudson Group Ltd
Bushell Street,
Preston,
Lancashire PR1 2SP
Tel: 0772 202202
Fax: 0772 889889

Just Fabrics
Burford Antique Centre,
Cheltenham Road,
Burford
Oxon OX8 4JA
Tel: 0993 82 3391

U.S.A.
ArtMark Fabric
480 Lancaster Pike
Frazer, PA 19355
Tel: 1-800-523-0362

Gige Interiors, Ltd (see *Curtain-hanging materials*)

Norbar Fabrics
1101 Lakeland Ave,
PO Box 528,
Bohemia,
NY 11716
Tel: 1-800-645-8501

SHEETING

U.K.
John Lewis Partnership (all branches) (see *Sewing Equipment*)

U.S.A.
George Matuk
37 West 26th Street
New York, NY 10010
Tel: 212-683-9242

COTTON LACE-MAKING

Lady Plunket
Rathmore Estate
Box 3
Chimanimani
Zimbabwe
Tel: 010 263 26 281

TABLE BASES, DRESSING AND TV TABLES

U.K.
The Dormy House
Sterling Park,
East Portway,
Andover, Hants SP10 3TZ
Tel: 0264 365 808

U.S.A.
Minic Custom Woodwork, Inc.
524 East 117th Street,
New York, NY 10035
Tel: 212-410-5500
Fax: 212-410-5533

Hoot Judkins
1142 Sutter Street,
San Francisco,CA 94109
Tel: 415 673 5454

CURTAIN-HANGING MATERIALS
Including the following: poles, heading
tapes, Span smocking tape, hooks, brass
acorns, 1⅛in lead weights, S-hooks,
screw-eyes, metal brackets, brass rings,
brass hooks and Kirsch curtain rails.

U.K.
Hunter and Hyland Ltd
201–205 Kingston Road,
Leatherhead,
Surrey KT22 7PB
Tel: 0372 378511
Fax: 0372 370038

U.S.A.
Gige Interiors, Ltd
170 S. Main Street,
Yardley, PA 19067
Tel: 215-493-8052

Graber Products Division
Springs Window Fashions
Middleton,
WI 53562
Tel: 1-800-356-9102

Kirsch Co
PO Box 370,
Sturges, MI 49091
Tel: 1-800-528-1407

HKH Design
24 Middlefield Drive
San Francisco
CA 94132
Tel: 415-564-2383

PERMANENT PLEATERS

U.K.
Ciment Pleating
39b Church Hill Road,
Church Hill, Walthamstow,
London E17 9RX
Tel: 081 520 0415

U.S.A.
SF Pleating
61 Greenpoint Avenue,
Brooklyn, NY 11222
Tel: 718-383-7950
and
425 Second Street
San Francisco
CA 94107
Tel: 415-982-3003

ROLLER BLINDS

U.K.
Decorshades
5 Brewery Mews Business Centre,
St John's Road,
Isleworth, Middlesex TW7 6PH
Tel: 081 847 1939

TRIMMINGS

G. J. Turner and Co (Trimmings Ltd)
Fitzroy House,
Abbot Street,
London E8 3DP
Tel: 071 254 8187
Fax: 071 254 8471

U.S.A.
M&J Trimmings
1008 Sixth Avenue,
New York,
NY 10018
Tel: 212-391-9072

CLEANERS

U.K.
Elite (Mr Bushky)
27 Churton Street,
London SW1
Tel: 071 834 0753

U.S.A.
Cleantex Process Co Inc
2335 12th Avenue,
New York, NY
Tel: 212-283-1200

DownRight Ltd
6101 16th Avenue,
Brooklyn, NY 11204
Tel: 718-232-2206

Photo Credits

The publisher and author would like to
thank the following for allowing their
photographs to be reproduced in this
book:

2 Fritz von der Schulenburg (Mark
   Hampton)
9 Simon Brown
10 Andreas von Einsiedel/EWA
   (Fowlkes)
11 Michael Dunne/EWA (Joanna Wood
   Design)
13 Andreas von Einsiedel/EWA (Erik
   Karson)
15 Osborne & Little (Elysium
   Collection)
19 Simon Brown
23 Fritz von der Schulenburg (Nina
   Campbell)
24 Rodney Hyett/EWA
25 Andreas von Einsiedel/EWA (Mrs
   Briggs)
26 EWA
27 Michael Dunne/EWA (Joanna Wood
   Design)

29 Fritz von der Schulenburg (George
   Spencer)
32 (top) Simon Brown; (bottom) Fritz
   von der Schulenburg (Meltons)
35 Fritz von der Schulenburg (Sissi
   Edmiston)
37 Fritz von der Schulenburg (Meltons)
41 Simon Brown
43 Fritz von der Schulenburg
44 IPC Magazines Ltd/Robert Harding
47 Marvic Textiles
49 Marvic Textiles
53 Osborne & Little (Artoise Stripe by
   Nina Campbell)
54 Michael Nicholson/EWA
55 IPC Magazines Ltd/Robert Harding
57 The Dormy House
58 Brian Harrison/Robert Harding
59 Simon Brown
61 Peter Wolosynski/EWA
63 Michael Dunne/EWA
67 Simon Brown
69 Fritz von der Schulenburg (David
   Hicks International)
71 Fritz von der Schulenburg (Meltons)
75 Trevor Richards Photography

76 Simon Brown
81 Fritz von der Schulenburg
83 Fritz von der Schulenburg (Bingham
   Land)
84 Behram Kapadia
90 Fritz von der Schulenburg
91 IPC Magazines Ltd/Robert Harding
95 IPC Magazines Ltd/Robert Harding
96 Peter Wolosynski/EWA
99 © Jane Churchill Limited
105 Fritz von der Schulenburg
106 IPC Magazines Ltd/Robert Harding
109 Joanna Trading
111 IPC Magazines Ltd/Robert Harding
112 Behram Kapadia
114 Fritz von der Schulenburg (John
   McCall)
115 IPC Magazines Ltd/Robert Harding
117 Fritz von der Schulenburg (Sissi
   Edmiston)
118 (top) Behram Kapadia; (bottom) Fritz
   von der Schulenburg (Conrad
   Jamieson)
119 Fritz von der Schulenburg (John
   McCall)
122 IPC Magazines Ltd/Robert Harding

INDEX